Bryant

Finding Out About

Everyday Things

Written by: **Eliot Humberstone**

Designed by: **Iain Ashman**

Consultant Editor: **Betty Root**

Illustrated by:
Louise Nevett
Basil Arm
Malcolm English
Bob Hersey
Gordon Wylie

Contents

Why does it rain?

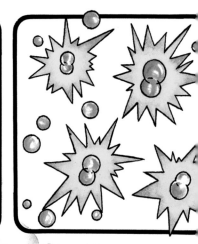

Every day millions of tiny drops of water rise up into the air, from rivers and seas.

When lots of these tiny drops of water float in the same part of the sky, they make a cloud.

If tiny drops bump into each other, they mix together and become bigger drops.

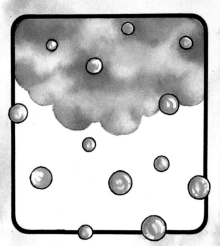

When these drops become heavy enough, they fall back to Earth. We call this rain.

In the country, rain soaks into the ground. In towns it goes down drains.

Eventually the rain runs back into the rivers and seas. It then rises again to the sky to make clou

ainbows

ake your own
ainbow

e best way to
nderstand rainbows is
 make one yourself.
 Put a glass of water
n a flat sheet of white
aper in front of a
unny window. You will
ee colored light on
he paper.

nside a
ain drop

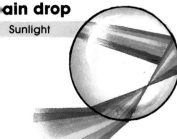

Raindrops in the sky
can act like the water
n your glass. Sunlight
divides into seven
colors inside a
aindrop.

Why you see
the colors

When there is a rainbow,
the raindrops reflect the
sunlight. White light from
the Sun is made up of
different colors.

Each color is bent by
a different amount, so
you can see them separately.
Red light is bent the most,
so it appears on the
outside of the rainbow.

Sunlight

raindrops

This is how the
light reaches
your eyes.

To see a rainbow,
you have to stand
in between the
sunlight and
the rain.

The colors of a
rainbow are always
in the same order—
red, orange,
yellow, green, blue,
indigo and violet.

3

Thunder and lightning

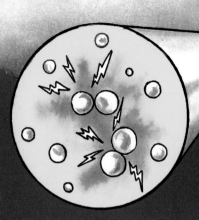

1 In the circle, you can see what happens in a cloud during a storm. Lots of tiny drops of water bump and rub against each other. This makes electricity in the cloud.

2 When the electricity leaves the cloud, it makes a spark that shoots towards the ground .
  This is what we call a flash of lightning.

3 Lightning sometimes strikes tall trees or buildings. This is because electricity travels better down a wet tree or building than through the air.

4 During a storm, you should stay away from anything that might be hit by lightning.
  The electricity in a flash of lightning is very dangerous.

5 The lightning shown here is forked lightning. If lightning jumps from one cloud to another cloud, it lights up the bottom of the clouds. This is called sheet lightning.

What is thunder?

A flash of lightning is very hot. When it goes through the air, it heats up the air around it.

As the air gets hot it takes up more room. It pushes away the air near the flash of lightning.

As the air is pushed away very quickly, it makes a loud sound. We call it thunder.

Why do you see the lightning before you hear the thunder?

Lightning and thunder happen at the same time, but light travels faster than sound through air.

You can find out how far away a storm is. Count the seconds between the lightning and the thunder.

Divide the number of seconds by three. This tells you how far away the storm is in kilometers.

Snow and ice

The air in a cloud is mixed with lots of tiny drops of water. When the drops get very cold, they turn into ice.

1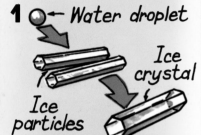

○← *Water droplet*

Ice particles

Ice crystal

The pieces of ice start very small. As they go through the air, more water freezes on them and they become bigger.

When the ice crystals are big enough, they join together and make snow flakes. If the snow flakes are heavy enough, they fall to the ground.

The North Pole and the South Pole are very cold. They are covered by ice and snow all through the year. At the North Pole there is no land—only very thick ice floating on the Arctic Ocean.

South Pole

Antarct

2 *Boiling point*

Steam

C. 100° 75° 50° 25° 0°

Water

Freezing point

Ice

Ice and steam are made of the same stuff as wat Water turns into ice when it gets colder than freezing point. When it is hotter than boiling poin water turns to steam.

...bergs are huge ...unks of ice that have ...oken away from the ...ges of icy places. They ...at in the sea until they ...elt in warm water.

Nine tenths of an iceberg are below the water.

6

In the winter we put a liquid called anti-freeze into car radiators. This does not freeze as easily as water and stops the pipes cracking.

4

5

This much water makes this much ice.

water   ice

...very cold nights, when ...mp air touches cold ...ngs such as leaves, it ...kes ice on them. This ... is called frost.

Icicles are made when water that is dripping freezes one drop at a time. Some icicles are very heavy and their points are very sharp.

If water in a pipe freezes, the pipe can crack. This is because the ice takes up more space than the water.

The Sun

All the daylight and all the hot weather on the Earth comes from the Sun.

The Sun shines all the time. Even when it is cloudy, it is there, though you cannot see it.

If you fly in an airplane during the daytime, you can see the Sun shining above the clouds.

This picture shows the Earth and the Sun from out in space. The Earth is always spinning around.

The Earth takes 24 hours to spin around once. This is why a day is 24 hours long.

When it is night-time for you, it is day-time for the people living on the other side of the Earth.

e Moon is a ball of
ck which goes around
e Earth. It takes a month
go around once.

The Moon is very dry and
rocky. It is covered with
powdery dust. Nothing
grows on the Moon.

The Moon has no light of
its own. It reflects light
from the Sun back to the
Earth.

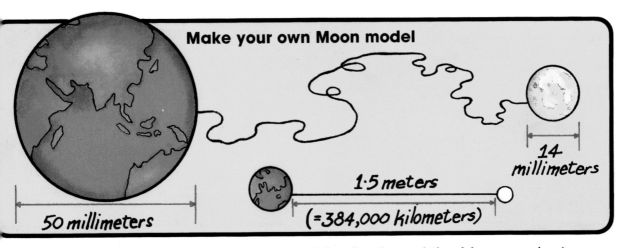

Make your own Moon model

50 millimeters

1·5 meters
(=384,000 kilometers)

14 millimeters

o see the difference between the sizes of the Earth and the Moon, make two
alls with plasticine. The sizes of the balls are shown above. The big one is the
arth. Now join the two balls with a piece of string 1.5 meters long. This will
ive you some idea of the distance from the Earth to the Moon.

The Seasons

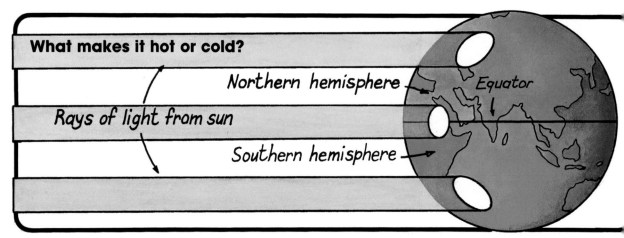

What makes it hot or cold?

Northern hemisphere

Equator

Rays of light from sun

Southern hemisphere

The Equator is an invisible line around the center of the Earth. It is usually hotte near the Equator. It gets colder the nearer you get to the Poles. This is becaus the sunrays that heat up the Earth are more spread out away from the Equato

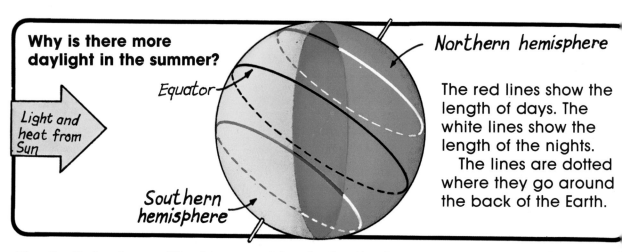

Why is there more daylight in the summer?

Light and heat from Sun

Equator

Northern hemisphere

Southern hemisphere

The red lines show the length of days. The white lines show the length of the nights.

The lines are dotted where they go around the back of the Earth.

The Earth is always tilted to one side. As the Earth moves around the Sun, this ti means that sometimes the Northern Hemisphere is leaning towards the Sun an sometimes the Southern Hemisphere is. When a hemisphere is leaning towards the Sun, it is summer there.

Why do the seasons change?

The changing seasons are caused by the changing position of the Earth in relation to the Sun. Each season lasts about three months. There are changes in weather, temperature and length of daylight.

1 Winter

In winter, the Sun's rays are spread out over a wider area of the Earth's surface. This is why it is colder.

2 Spring

By springtime, the Earth has moved around the Sun. That is why the days are longer and the Sun's rays make it warmer.

4 Autumn

In autumn, the Earth has moved around and the weather begins to get colder and the days get shorter.

3 Summer

In summer, the Sun's rays can be hot, because the Earth is leaning towards the Sun. Parts of the Earth now nearest the Sun become warm.

Stars and planets

The Stars

On a clear night you can see thousands of stars. They are suns, like our Sun. They look much smaller because they are very, very much farther away. Stars are made of hot, gases that burn very brightly.

The nine planets that go round our Sun are much smaller than stars.

Our part of the Universe is called the Solar System. This picture shows what it would look like from outer space.

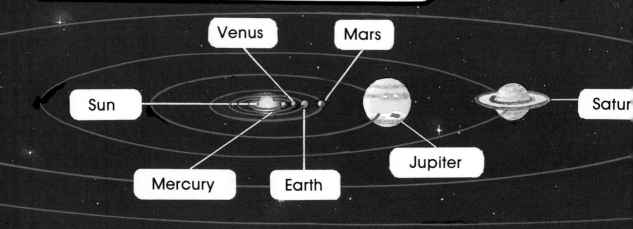

Venus

Mars

Sun

Satur

Mercury

Earth

Jupiter

The Planets

These pictures are not drawn to scale.

Mercury

Venus

Earth

Moon

Mars

Mercury is the closest planet to the Sun. It has no atmosphere.

In the morning and the evening, Venus looks as bright as a star in the sky.

Earth is the only planet where we are certain that life does exist.

Mars is the o planet that a spacecraft h landed on.

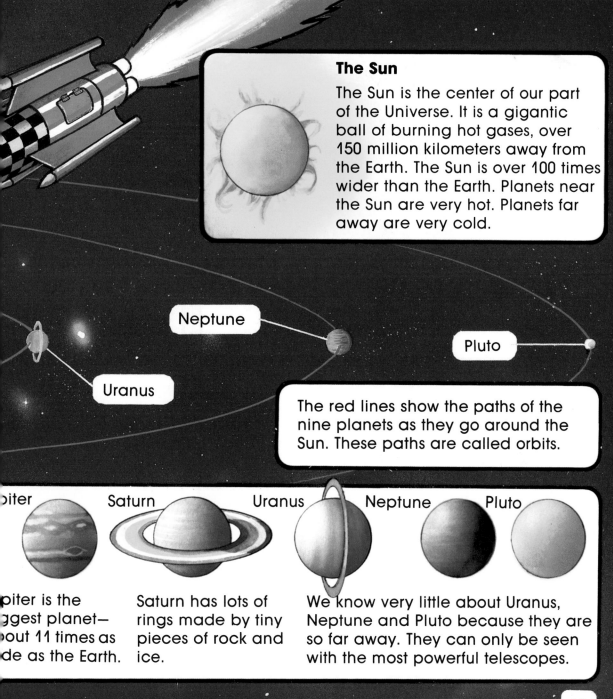

The Sun

The Sun is the center of our part of the Universe. It is a gigantic ball of burning hot gases, over 150 million kilometers away from the Earth. The Sun is over 100 times wider than the Earth. Planets near the Sun are very hot. Planets far away are very cold.

Neptune

Pluto

Uranus

The red lines show the paths of the nine planets as they go around the Sun. These paths are called orbits.

Jupiter

Saturn

Uranus

Neptune

Pluto

Jupiter is the biggest planet— about 11 times as wide as the Earth.

Saturn has lots of rings made by tiny pieces of rock and ice.

We know very little about Uranus, Neptune and Pluto because they are so far away. They can only be seen with the most powerful telescopes.

Volcanoes

1

The Earth is made of three sections. The outside is called the crust. It is thin and brittle. The inside is made of soft rock. This is called the mantle.

The center of the Earth is the core. Scientists believe that the rock there is so hot that it is liquid.

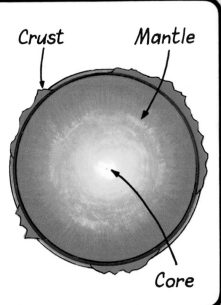

Crust

Mantle

Core

2

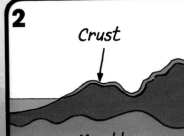

Crust

Mantle

The Earth's crust is very thin compared with the rest of the Earth. It varies in thickness from 8 kilometers to 64 kilometers.

3

Earth's crust

The mantle under the crust of the Earth is made of hot soft rock. This moves around all the time.

4

Magma

This soft rock is called magma. It can be hot enough to melt the rock above it.

5

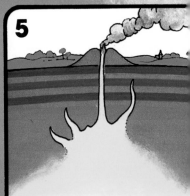

Sometimes the hot magma breaks through a thin weak part of the crust. This is the start of a volcano.

Some volcanoes do nothing for hundreds of years. Then suddenly the hot magma shoots out of the crater. This is called erupting.

The magma cools as it comes to the top. It flows out of the crust and is called lava. It flows down the sides of the volcano and becomes hard like rock.

Some of the lava is full of bubbles of gas. This becomes rock called pumice. Because of the gas bubbles, it can float.

9 Many volcanic eruptions can be heard for hundreds of kilometers. In 1883, a volcano called Krakatoa exploded in Indonesia.

The noise could be heard 4,700 kilometers away in Australia.

10 The hole which is made by the hot magma breaking through the crust is called a crater.

11 During each eruption lava builds up in layers on the sides of the volcano. This is how the cone shape is formed.

15

Close to the ground

Look carefully under stones, inside flowers and between the grass. You will find lots of creatures close to the ground.

Worms eat rotting plants. The remains of the plants pass through their bodies into the soil. This improves the soil and helps the plants grow.

This is a side view of the ground, just below the top of the soil.

Worms sometimes pull leaves down into the ground to eat.

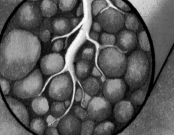

Soil is made of lots of tiny pieces of powdered rocks and rotting plants. Good soil has gaps of air between the particles to allow plant roots to grow.

Worm watching

Put a piece of board over a patch of grass. Leave it for a few weeks and then look underneath.

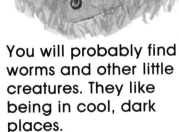

You will probably find worms and other little creatures. They like being in cool, dark places.

ugs and snails love to
at young plants. The
est time to see slugs
nd snails is at night
hen it is cool and
ark.

ug⟩ ⟩Snail

You can often find
woodlice on the
bark of old twigs.
They eat the rotting
wood.

The top of a toadstool
carries its seeds, called
spores. Under the ground, a
toadstool is made of lots of
fine white strands.

Woodlouse ⟩

The roots of some trees
send out runners that
go up to the top of the
ground to start another
tree.

loles live in nests of
rass under the ground.
ey build tunnels and
atch worms to eat.

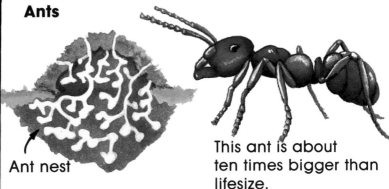

Ants

Ant nest

This ant is about
ten times bigger than
lifesize.

Ants live in large groups underground. They
sometimes build small mounds of earth above
their nests and bring their eggs up to the
mounds to be warmed by the sunshine.

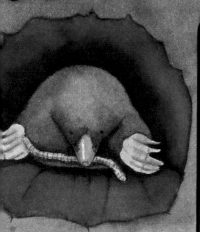

How flowers grow

These pages show you how a buttercup grows. Most plants grow in the same way. All flowers make seeds from which new plants grow.

Flowers need pollen from other flowers of the same kind before they can make new seeds. Pollen is carried by insects or by the wind.

Buttercup seeds are inside the fruits. The fruit is only as big as a pinhead.

Fruits

Buttercup

The seed is in here.

Root

Before it can turn into a new plant, the seed needs water. Rain makes the seed swell. It starts to grow.

The seed puts out a tiny root with little hairs. The root grows down into the ground.

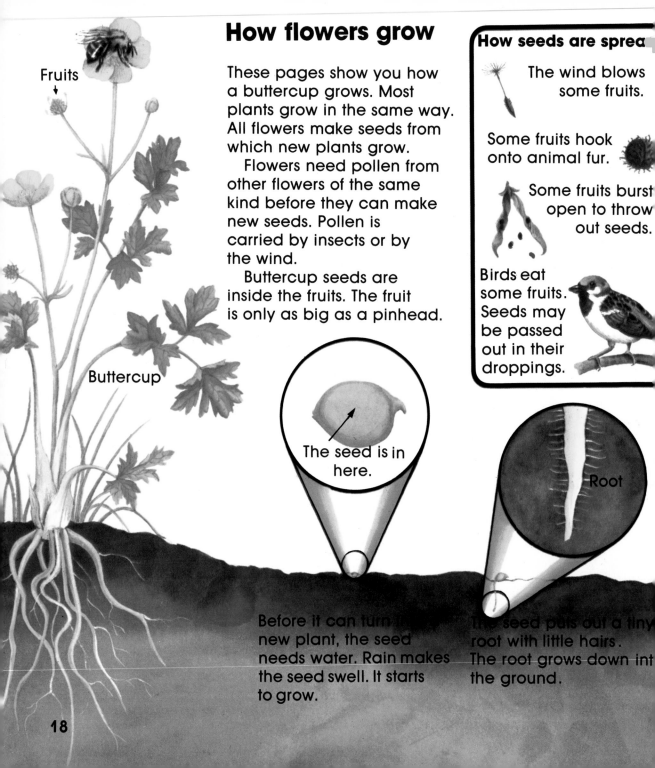

How seeds are spread

The wind blows some fruits.

Some fruits hook onto animal fur.

Some fruits burst open to throw out seeds.

Birds eat some fruits. Seeds may be passed out in their droppings.

Watch a seed grow

Roll up a piece of blotting paper. Put it in a jam jar so it presses out against the sides. Put a bean half way down the jar between the glass and the paper.

Now fill the bottom third of the jar with water. After a day or two look at the roots through a magnifying glass. Beans grow fast, so a shoot will soon grow out of the jar.

aterpillars, slugs and snails like to at young shoots. Young plants an also be damaged by bad eather.

root hairs take in water and nerals from the soil. on, a little shoot comes out of e seed.

The leaves grow. The light helps the plant to make food.

Later, flowers grow on top of the stalks. They start to make seeds that will grow into other plants.

19

Trees

Trees are the biggest living things in the world, and they also live longest.

Leaves

The leaves make the food for the tree. They need light to make food from water and a gas in the air called carbon dioxide.

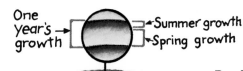

One year's growth → ← Summer growth ← Spring growth

Bark

The thick stem of a tree is called the trunk. This is covered by bark. The bark stops a tree from getting too hot or too cold.

Growth rings

When a tree is cut down, you can see rings on the inside. The dark wood has grown each summer. The lighter wood grew each spring. Count the darker rings and you will see roughly how old the tree is.

Roots

The roots of a tree go a long way down into the ground. This helps the tree to stand up. The roots absorb water from the soil so that the tree can grow.

Flowers

Many trees have flowers but some are hard to see.

Insects or wind carry pollen from one flower to another. This makes the seeds for new trees.

Fruit and seeds

Some trees have fruits like apples and oranges. The seeds are inside these fruits. Nuts are large seeds which have hard outsides.

Bark rubbing

Tape a piece of thin paper to the trunk of a tree. Rub gently over the paper with a wax crayon. Be careful not to tear the paper.

You can learn to recognize different trees by looking at their bark carefully. If you make bark rubbings, you can keep the different patterns in a book.

Rivers

Rivers start off as small streams. They get bigger as they collect more water from the countryside they flow through.

The water in rivers com from rain or melted sno

Rivers carve out the lan they flow over. If rivers flow fast, they make de river beds.

Hydro-electric power stations are built on lar rivers. Inside their dams the water from the river made to drive an engir that makes electricity.

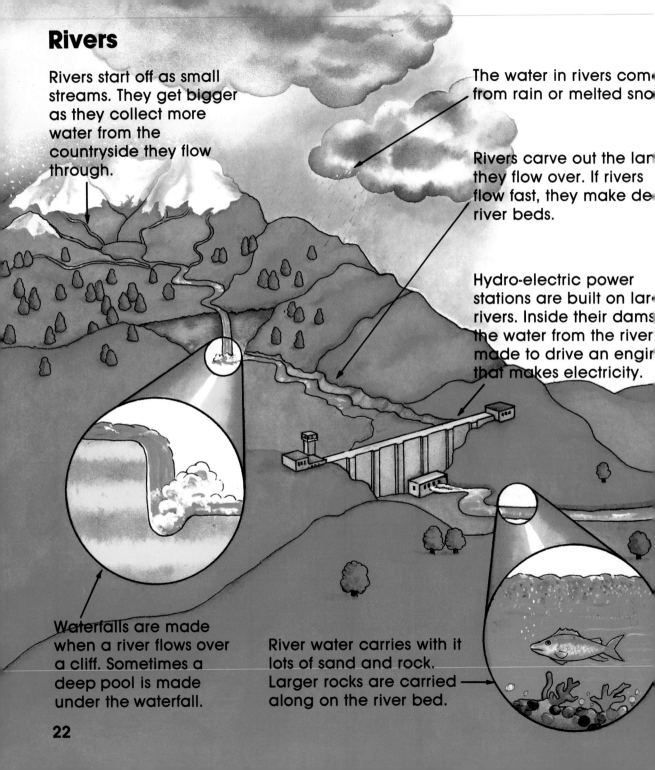

Waterfalls are made when a river flows over a cliff. Sometimes a deep pool is made under the waterfall.

River water carries with it lots of sand and rock. Larger rocks are carried along on the river bed.

22

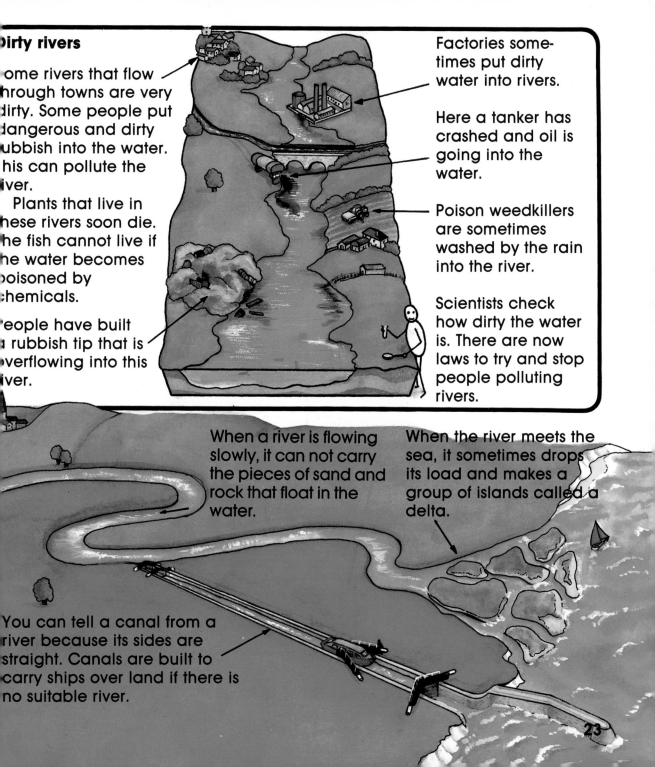

Dirty rivers

Some rivers that flow through towns are very dirty. Some people put dangerous and dirty rubbish into the water. This can pollute the river.

Plants that live in these rivers soon die. The fish cannot live if the water becomes poisoned by chemicals.

People have built a rubbish tip that is overflowing into this river.

Factories sometimes put dirty water into rivers.

Here a tanker has crashed and oil is going into the water.

Poison weedkillers are sometimes washed by the rain into the river.

Scientists check how dirty the water is. There are now laws to try and stop people polluting rivers.

When a river is flowing slowly, it can not carry the pieces of sand and rock that float in the water.

When the river meets the sea, it sometimes drops its load and makes a group of islands called a delta.

You can tell a canal from a river because its sides are straight. Canals are built to carry ships over land if there is no suitable river.

The beach

If you look carefully on the bea
you can see lots of interesting
plants and animals.

Rock pools are made by
the sea water that is left
behind after the tide has
gone out. You can find
seaweed, crabs and small
fish living in rock pools.

Near to the sea, bi
waves break up
large rocks into sm
rocks. The sea rubs
them against each
other. After a long
time, they become
rounded pebbles.

Look carefully at
the sand. It is
made of lots of
tiny pieces of
rock and broken
bits of sea shells.

When the tide comes in, it brings dead seaweed, shells and rubbish. It leaves all this on the sand and it makes a line on the beach. It is called a strand line.

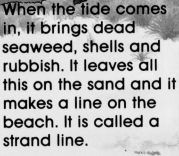

Shells are the outside hard cases of small molluscs. Some are spiral shaped, like snails. Others are two pieces hinged together.

Seaweeds grow on rocks and other things that are covered by the sea at high tide. Sea weeds stand up when the sea covers them. Some have air in pockets that helps them float.

Things that look like worms made of sand are worm casts. They are made by lugworms that dig in the sand. The worms eat the sand and pass it out of their bodies to make the casts.

Waves

Most waves are made by the wind. When there is no wind, there are no waves.

When the wind starts, small ripples appear on the top of the sea.

When the wind blows harder, it pushes the ripples until they becon waves.

This is a side view of a slice of the sea and the beach

How waves break

Near the beach, the water underneath the wave drags back on the land and is slowed down.

This makes the top of the wave topple forward and break on the beach.

...ves are very strong. ...y can carve out bays ...the coastline and ...eak away rocks to ...ake caves.

Sometimes, after many years, waves break through the back of the cave. This makes an arch.

After more time, the arch falls down. A pillar of strong rock, called a stack, is left standing.

...e biggest wave ... the world

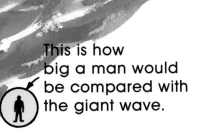

...e biggest wave in the ...orld happened in the ...cific Ocean in 1933. ...e wave was 34 ...eters high.

This is how big a man would be compared with the giant wave.

Wave power

These machines go up and down with the waves. They make electricity. This can be taken ashore by a cable.

27

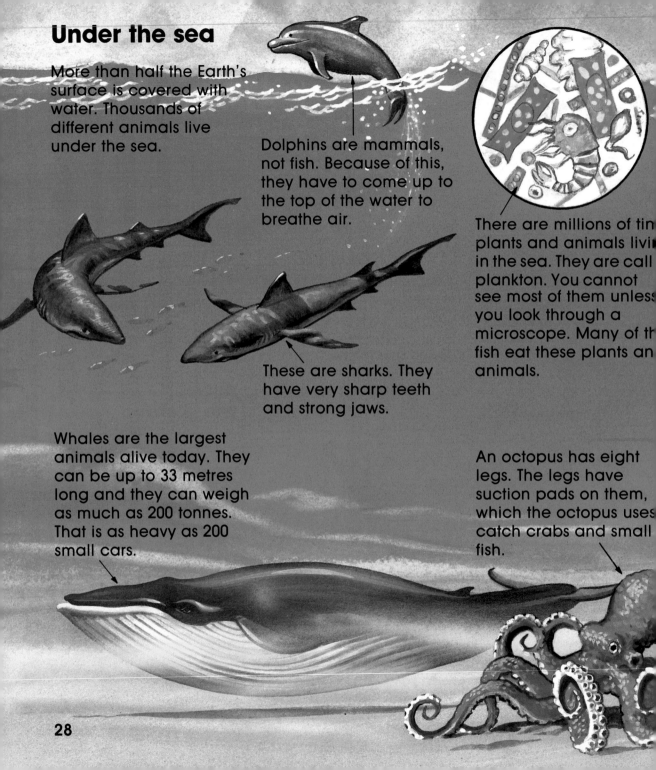

Under the sea

More than half the Earth's surface is covered with water. Thousands of different animals live under the sea.

Dolphins are mammals, not fish. Because of this, they have to come up to the top of the water to breathe air.

There are millions of tin[...] plants and animals livi[...] in the sea. They are call[...] plankton. You cannot see most of them unless you look through a microscope. Many of th[...] fish eat these plants an[...] animals.

These are sharks. They have very sharp teeth and strong jaws.

Whales are the largest animals alive today. They can be up to 33 metres long and they can weigh as much as 200 tonnes. That is as heavy as 200 small cars.

An octopus has eight legs. The legs have suction pads on them, which the octopus uses [...] catch crabs and small fish.

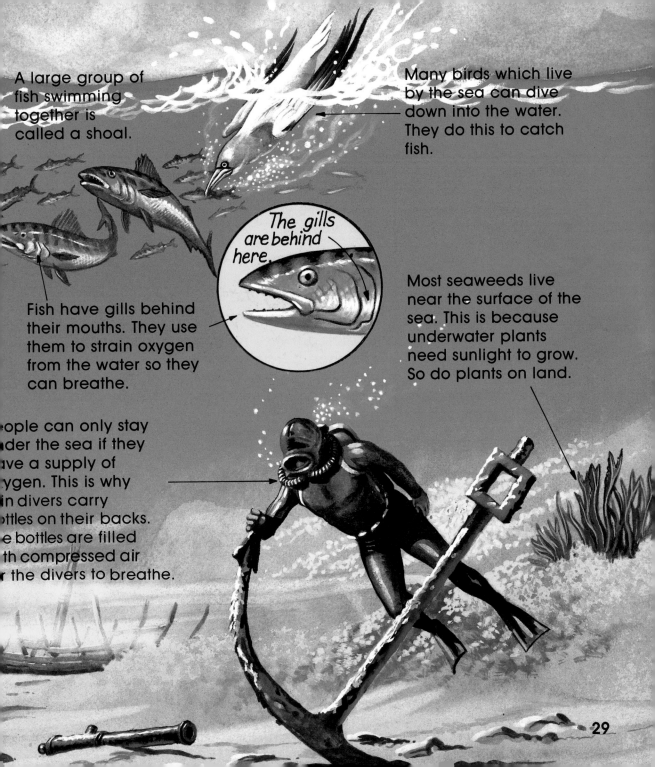

A large group of fish swimming together is called a shoal.

Many birds which live by the sea can dive down into the water. They do this to catch fish.

The gills are behind here.

Fish have gills behind their mouths. They use them to strain oxygen from the water so they can breathe.

Most seaweeds live near the surface of the sea. This is because underwater plants need sunlight to grow. So do plants on land.

...ople can only stay ...der the sea if they ...ave a supply of ...ygen. This is why ...n divers carry ...ottles on their backs. ...e bottles are filled ...th compressed air ...r the divers to breathe.

29

Measuring things

How to measure exactly

If you want to measure things exactly you will need a ruler or a tape measure. We usually use the metric system to measure.

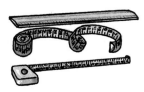

A millimeter is very small, only as long as this line⊙. There are ten millimeters in one centimeter. The ruler on this page is divided into centimeters. There are 100 centimeters in one meter.

The tail of the kite goes round this page. The distance between each bow of ribbon is five centimeters. How long is the tail?

The answer is on page 32.

Using your feet

If you do not have a ruler or a tape measure you cannot measure things exactly, but you can measure them roughly. Try using your own feet. Make certain the toe of one foot always touches the heel of the other. If you measure your shoe you can work out exact distances this way.

Using your hands

Stretch out your hand and measure the distance between the tip of your thumb and your little finger. You can then always use your hand to measure distances roughly.

Measure across your hand from thumb to little finger

Using your arms

Stretch out your arm and measure from the tip of your nose to the tip of your longest finger. When you know this distance, you can measure cloth or a length of string.

Measure from you nose to the tip of your middle finger

Using string to measure things

If things are a difficult shape to measure, try using a piece of string.

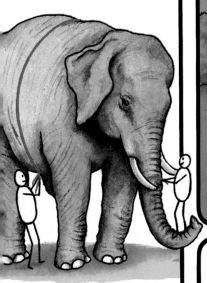

Find the shortest road through the park on this map.

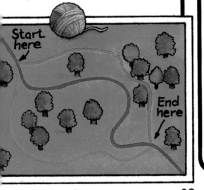

Using a twig to measure a tree

With a tape measure, mark off one metre on a tree trunk. Start on the ground. Walk away from the tree until you can see all of it. Find a straight twig. Hold this out in front of you.

One meter mark

Move your thumb up the twig until it is in line with the mark on the tree. Mark the twig where your thumb is. Then see how many times the length of the twig above the thumb goes into the height of the tree. This will tell you roughly the height of the tree in meters.

Kite Puzzle

The answer is on page 32.

Will the kite fit into the box? You can use a ruler to help you check.

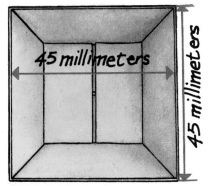

45 millimeters

45 millimeters

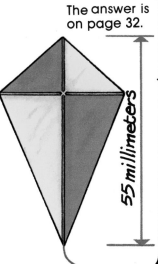

55 millimeters

Answer on page 32.

Outdoor Quiz

1 What are clouds made of?
   (1) Air (2) Water (3) Air and water.
2 Light and sound both take time to travel through the air. Which travels faster?
3 Why do water pipes crack in the winter sometimes?
4 How long does it take for the Moon to go round the Earth? (1) One day (2) One month (3) One year.
5 How long does it take for the Earth to go round the Sun? (1) 24 hours (2) One month (3) One year.
6 How many planets are there going around the Sun?
7 What is the center of the Earth called?
8 Why do ants sometimes build mounds of Earth above their nests?
9 What is sand made of?
10 What are worm casts?
11 What makes the waves?
12 What are the largest animals alive today?
13 How many legs does an octopus have?
14 Why does a fish have gills?
15 What is the name of a large group of fish?
16 Why do dolphins have to come to the top of the sea to breathe air?

Answers to questions about Measuring things:

The tail of the kite is one meter long.

The shortest road on the map of the park is the orange road.

Yes, the kite will fit into the box, like this:

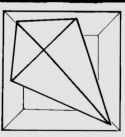

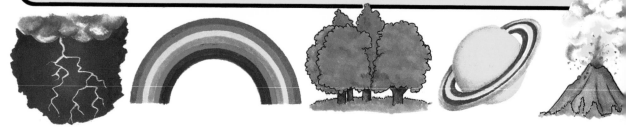

Part 2
THINGS THAT GO

Written by: **Eliot Humberstone**

Designed by: **Iain Ashman**

Consultant Editor: **Betty Root**

Science Consultants: **Anthony Wilson** **Aubrey Tulley**

Researcher: **Nigel Flynn**

Illustrated by:

Basil Arm
Louise Nevett
Eric Smart
Graham Smith
Clive Spong
Mike Roffe
Gordon Wylie
Guy Smith

Contents

33

Ferry boats

The boat in this picture is a ferry. It can carry lots of passengers, cars and trucks. They drive on at the front and drive off at the back.

This is the funnel. Waste gas from the ship's diesel engines comes out here.

The small boat on the top deck are life boats. They ca be lowered over the side it the ship starts to sink.

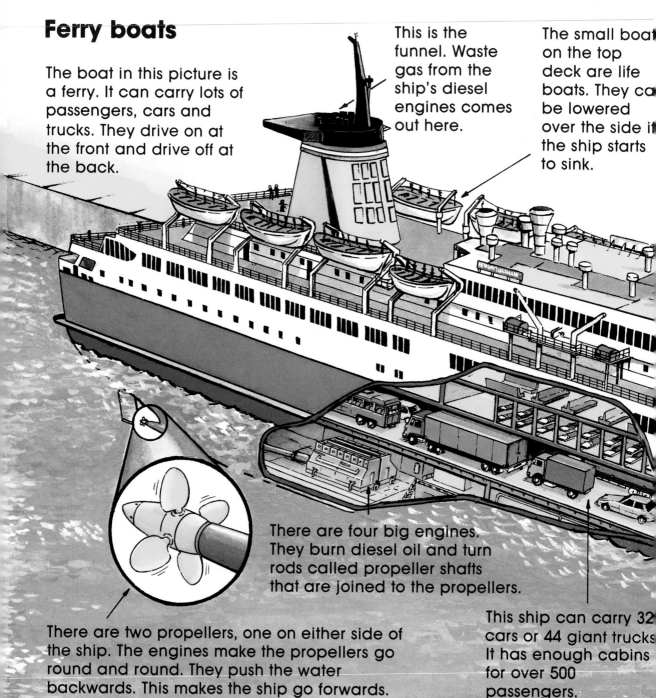

There are four big engines. They burn diesel oil and turn rods called propeller shafts that are joined to the propellers.

There are two propellers, one on either side of the ship. The engines make the propellers go round and round. They push the water backwards. This makes the ship go forwards.

This ship can carry 32 cars or 44 giant trucks It has enough cabins for over 500 passengers.

34

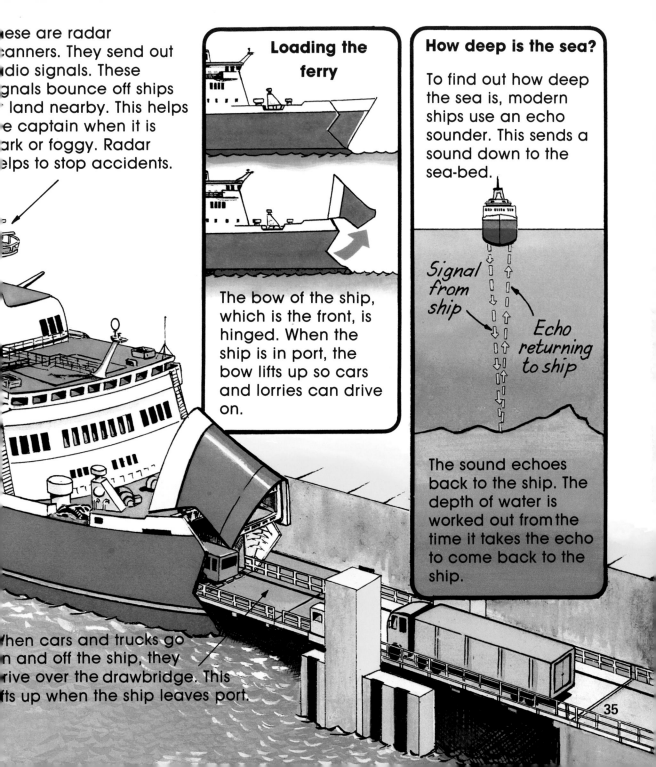

ese are radar
:anners. They send out
idio signals. These
ignals bounce off ships
land nearby. This helps
e captain when it is
ark or foggy. Radar
elps to stop accidents.

Loading the ferry

The bow of the ship, which is the front, is hinged. When the ship is in port, the bow lifts up so cars and lorries can drive on.

How deep is the sea?

To find out how deep the sea is, modern ships use an echo sounder. This sends a sound down to the sea-bed.

Signal from ship

Echo returning to ship

The sound echoes back to the ship. The depth of water is worked out from the time it takes the echo to come back to the ship.

/hen cars and trucks go
n and off the ship, they
rive over the drawbridge. This
ts up when the ship leaves port.

35

Sailing boats

These small sailing boats are called dinghies. If you sail in a dinghy you need to keep close to the coast as it is not safe to go out in rough seas.

The sail of a boat is made of light nylon material. By moving the boom, the sail can be turned around so it catches the wind. The wind pushes the boat along.

This is called a boom. It can swing round to either side of the boat. This helps the sail to catch the wind.

Steering the boat

The tiller is for steering the boat. It is fixed to the rudder. When you pull the tiller one way, it pushes the rudder in the opposite direction.

Water pushing against the rudder helps turn the boat around.

The center board is below the boat. It is a flat board that goes into the water. This stops the wind blowing the boat along sideways.

In the past

In the past, large sailing ships used to carry goods and passengers all around the world. Some were 100 meters long and some had as many as five masts. They needed a crew of up to 50 people to work all the sails.

Catamarans and trimarans

Most boats have only one hull. It is smooth and pointed to go through the water easily.

Hull

Catamaran

Trimaran

Some boats, called catamarans, have two hulls. Others, called trimarans, have three hulls. These boats are faster than ordinary boats of the same size and they do not tip over very easily.

Submarines

Submarines have large tanks called ballast tanks. These can be filled with water or air to make the submarine go down or up.

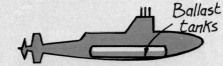

To go down, the ballast tanks are filled with water. This makes the submarine heavy, so it sinks.

Ballast tank

In order to stay at the same depth, the water in the tanks is moved around to different tanks, to keep the submarine steady.

Ballast tanks

To come up, the ballast tanks are filled with air. This makes the submarine light so it rises.

This small submarine is called a submersible. It is used for repairing oil rigs and for checking cables on the sea-bed. The submersible is put on a boat and taken out to sea. Then it is lowered over the side.

This is a mechanical arm. It can pick things up from the sea-bed.

The ballast tanks are in here.

Two little motors at the front steer the submersible.

Bright spotlights are needed to light up the dark sea-bed.

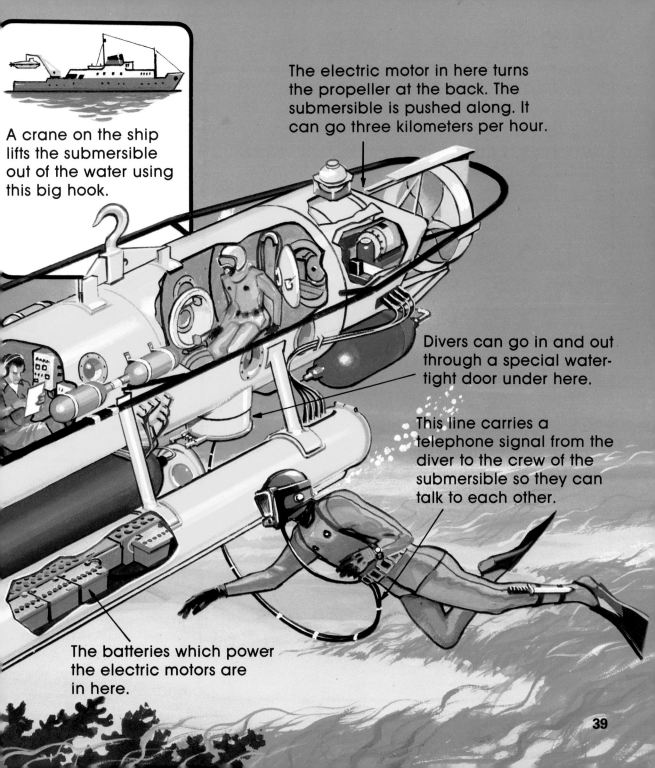

A crane on the ship lifts the submersible out of the water using this big hook.

The electric motor in here turns the propeller at the back. The submersible is pushed along. It can go three kilometers per hour.

Divers can go in and out through a special water-tight door under here.

This line carries a telephone signal from the diver to the crew of the submersible so they can talk to each other.

The batteries which power the electric motors are in here.

Hydrofoils

A hydrofoil is a boat that can move on the top of the water. It is raised up on metal wings called foils. It goes much faster than an ordinary boat because most of its body presses against air, not against water.

The foils can be lifted and lowered on these legs

When it is moving slowly, a hydrofoil floats on the water like an ordinary boat. As it goes faster, the foils are lowered into the water. Water going over the foils pushes them up and so the boat rises.

When it is going very fast, most of the hull is out of the water. Only the foils are in the water. The engine is above the middle of the back foil.

This hydrofoil can carry up to **245** passengers. Hydrofoils are used for going across short piece of sea. They can go twic as fast as ordinary ferries.

Engine

Water shoots out here

The engine in this hydrofoil sucks in water, turns it round and round and then shoots it out th back. This pushes the boat along.

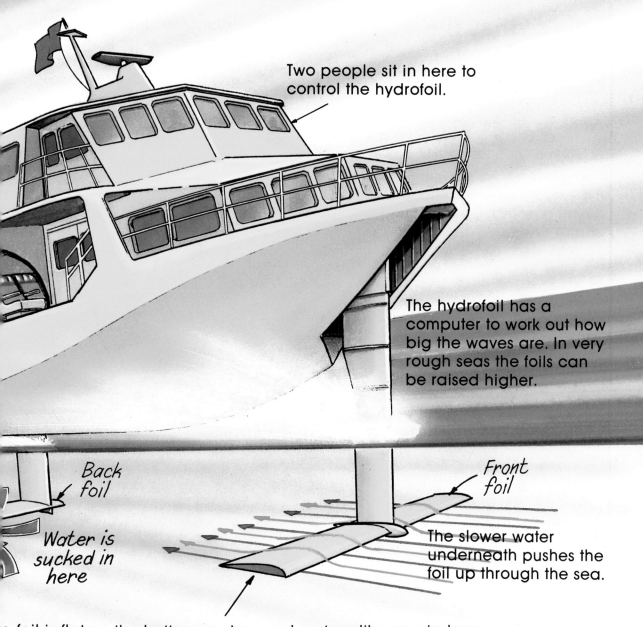

Two people sit in here to control the hydrofoil.

The hydrofoil has a computer to work out how big the waves are. In very rough seas the foils can be raised higher.

Back foil

Water is sucked in here

Front foil

The slower water underneath pushes the foil up through the sea.

e foil is flat on the bottom and curved on top, like an airplane ng. Water going over the top of the foil has to go faster than the ater going below. Water going past the foil lifts it up in the same way at moving air keeps an airplane flying.

How planes fly

The airplane on these pages is a small two-seater plane. It is the kind of plane you learn to fly in.

This is one of the elevators. If the pilot turns them up, the plane goes up. If the pilot turns them down, the plane goes down.

The rudder is for steering the plane. When air rushes against the rudder, it turns the plane the way the rudder is pointing.

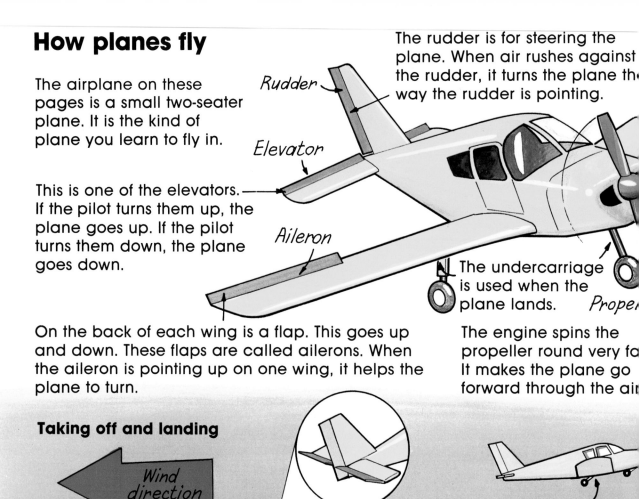

Rudder

Elevator

Aileron

The undercarriage is used when the plane lands.

Proper

On the back of each wing is a flap. This goes up and down. These flaps are called ailerons. When the aileron is pointing up on one wing, it helps the plane to turn.

The engine spins the propeller round very fa It makes the plane go forward through the air

Taking off and landing

Wind direction

Elevators raised

The undercarriag folds up

Before they can take off, planes must go fast along the ground. This makes the air rush past their wings.

To make the plane climb, the pilot must raise the elevator flaps at the back of the plane. This helps the air underneath the wings push up on them so the plane is supported in the air.

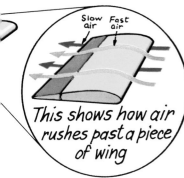

This shows how air rushes past a piece of wing

'ings are usually flat nderneath and curved n top. This makes air go ister over the top, so ere is less air there. The ings are pushed up by ir from below trying to I the space above em.

How wings work

Blow over the top of the paper

The best way to see how an airplane wing works is to try this test. Blow hard just above a sheet of paper. Your breath is like the fast air above a wing. There is less air on top, so the paper is lifted up by the air below.

Elevators lowered

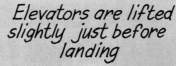

Elevators are lifted slightly just before landing

The pilot turns off the engine when the plane has landed

come down, the pilot wers the elevators. Air ushes against them and e plane goes down.

As the plane comes down, the pilot lowers the undercarriage. The elevator flaps are then lifted slightly. This raises the plane so that the wheels touch down first.

Jumbo jets

The last two pages showed you how all planes fly. Jet airliners are large planes. Many people can fly in them. They can go a long way.

The cockpit is right in the front of the plane. The pilot, the co-pilot and the flight engineer sit there.

Some Jumbos can carr over 400 passengers. During the flight, they can watch films.

Jumbo jets are the biggest passenger planes in the world. People can go up a spiral staircase to the top deck.

There are four engines on a Jumbo jet, two under each wing.

How the engine works

A jet engine takes in air at the front and pushes it very fast through the back. When the air is forced out through the back, the plane is pushed forwards.

The fan spins round very fast and takes in air from the front. It shoots the air out very fast at the back.

Fuel like gas mixes with air and burns in here. Hot gas shoot out at the back push the plane forwar

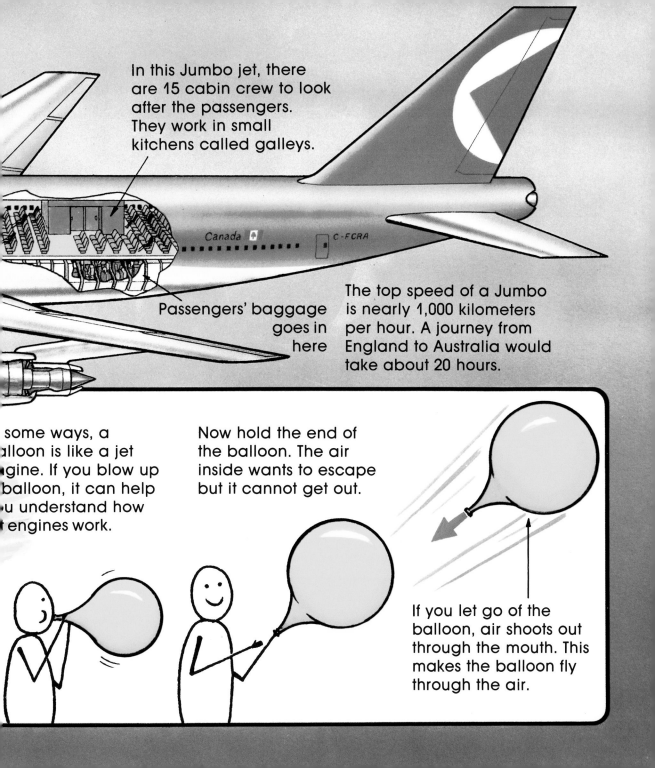

In this Jumbo jet, there are 15 cabin crew to look after the passengers. They work in small kitchens called galleys.

Passengers' baggage goes in here

The top speed of a Jumbo is nearly 1,000 kilometers per hour. A journey from England to Australia would take about 20 hours.

Canada C-FCRA

In some ways, a balloon is like a jet engine. If you blow up a balloon, it can help you understand how jet engines work.

Now hold the end of the balloon. The air inside wants to escape but it cannot get out.

If you let go of the balloon, air shoots out through the mouth. This makes the balloon fly through the air.

Balloons

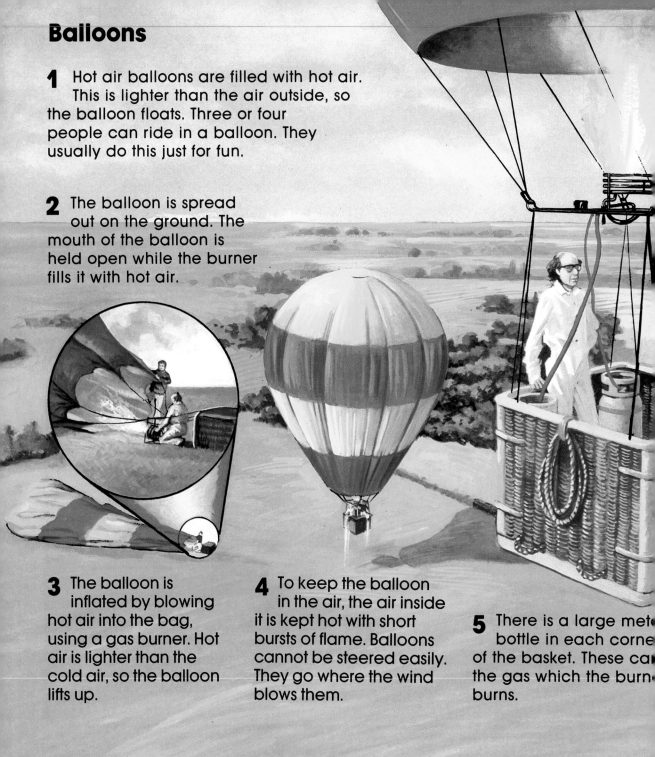

1 Hot air balloons are filled with hot air. This is lighter than the air outside, so the balloon floats. Three or four people can ride in a balloon. They usually do this just for fun.

2 The balloon is spread out on the ground. The mouth of the balloon is held open while the burner fills it with hot air.

3 The balloon is inflated by blowing hot air into the bag, using a gas burner. Hot air is lighter than the cold air, so the balloon lifts up.

4 To keep the balloon in the air, the air inside it is kept hot with short bursts of flame. Balloons cannot be steered easily. They go where the wind blows them.

5 There is a large mete bottle in each corne of the basket. These ca the gas which the burne burns.

6 The pilot uses the burner to control the height of the balloon. The hotter he makes the air inside, the higher the basket rises.

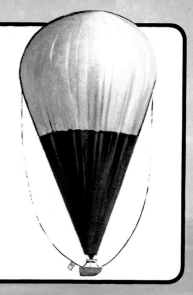

Across the ocean

In 1978 three Americans made the first successful crossing of the Atlantic Ocean in a balloon, called Double Eagle. The journey from the U.S.A. to France took six days.

Double Eagle was filled with a gas called helium, which is much lighter than air.

10 On the ground the pilot pulls a cord attached to a panel on the balloon. This opens up and the rest of the hot air in the balloon can escape.

7 Steel wires join the basket to the balloon.

8 The balloon is made of nylon. The basket is made of willow branches woven together. This is strong and light.

9 A hot air balloon will go wherever the wind blows it. To come down, the pilot turns off the burner. The air inside the balloon gets cool and so it gets heavier.

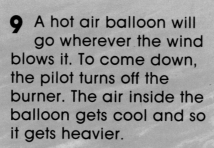

47

1 Earlier rockets could only be used once. The Space Shuttle can be used many times. It takes scientific instruments up into space to study the stars and the planets.

Hot gas rushes out here

Liquid oxygen tank

Fuel and oxygen mix and burn in here

Fuel tank

Inside a rocket, fuel like gas burns with oxygen to make very hot gases. The gases expand and rush out through the back. When this happens the rocket is pushed forward.

4 Space Shuttle can orbit the Earth for as long as 30 days without landing. It can fly 160 kilometers above the Earth.

5 The three main engines push the Shuttle up into space. Two smaller ones are used to steer the Space Shuttle and to point it back to Earth at the end

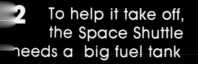

2 To help it take off, the Space Shuttle needs a big fuel tank

3 After eight minutes the rockets fall back to Earth. The fuel tank drops

ane. The living area is
der the flight control deck.

This is a solar panel. It
takes in light from the
n and turns it into
ectricity. Machines that
e Shuttle carries can
e the electricity.

Living quarters

10 When the Space
Shuttle comes back to
Earth, it glows red hot
from air friction.

USA

The top of the Space
Shuttle opens up. Then
e scientific instruments
n study the parts of
ter space which cannot

9 The part of the Space
Shuttle that opens up
can also be used to
carry satellites into
space. The satellite
would leave the plane
and could be picked up

11 The Space Shuttle land
just like an ordinary
plane.

Helicopters

Helicopters take off straight up into the air. They can fly forwards, backwards or sideways. They can also hover in one place.

The pictures below show you how the pilot can control a helicopter by tilting the blades.

The engine is at the top of a helicopter in the middle. It makes a rod spin round very fast. This turns the blades round.

Helicopters like this can go as fast as 250 kilometers per hour.

Fast air

Slower air

A helicopter blade is shaped like the wing of an airplane. It is curved on top and flat on the bottom.

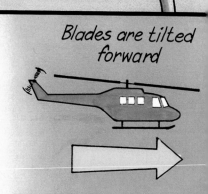

1 Going up

The engine turns the blades round very fast. This lifts the helicopter into the air. The blades are level.

Blades are level so helicopter rises

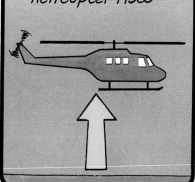

2 Going forward

When the pilot tilts the blades down at the front, the helicopter flies forward. The blades go round very fast. This pulls the helicopter along.

Blades are tilted forward

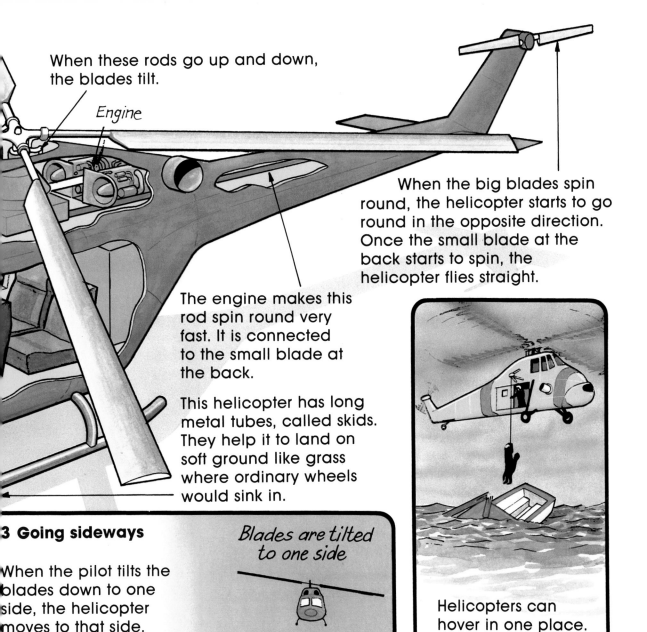

When these rods go up and down, the blades tilt.

Engine

The engine makes this rod spin round very fast. It is connected to the small blade at the back.

This helicopter has long metal tubes, called skids. They help it to land on soft ground like grass where ordinary wheels would sink in.

When the big blades spin round, the helicopter starts to go round in the opposite direction. Once the small blade at the back starts to spin, the helicopter flies straight.

3 Going sideways

When the pilot tilts the blades down to one side, the helicopter moves to that side. Ordinary planes cannot fly sideways like this.

Blades are tilted to one side

Helicopters can hover in one place. This helps them to rescue people from the sea.

Trains

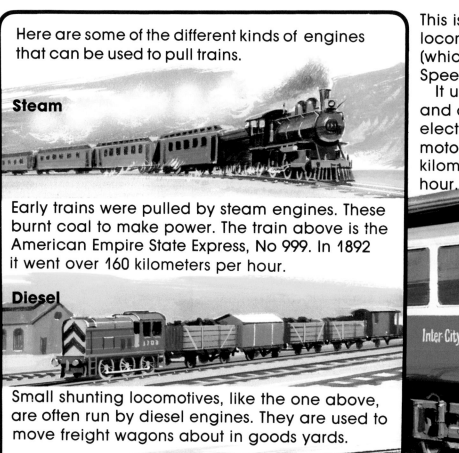

Here are some of the different kinds of engines that can be used to pull trains.

Steam

Early trains were pulled by steam engines. These burnt coal to make power. The train above is the American Empire State Express, No 999. In 1892 it went over 160 kilometers per hour.

Diesel

Small shunting locomotives, like the one above, are often run by diesel engines. They are used to move freight wagons about in goods yards.

Electric

Some electric trains take their electricity from overhead wires. This one is Japanese. It is called the Bullet Train. It can go over 250 kilometers per hour.

Inside a diesel electric locomotive

This is a modern British locomotive called an H (which stands for 'High Speed Train').

It uses a diesel engine and a generator to make electricity for the electric motors. HSTs can go 200 kilometers per hour.

Inter-City

3

3 The motors

The wheels are turned by electric motors just above the axle. They run on the electricity from the generator.

The engine

e diesel engine is very powerful.
s stronger than a bus or truck
gine. It runs off diesel fuel, which
like gasoline.

2 The generator

A rod that comes from the engine to
the generator spins round very fast.
Inside the generator, this spinning
movement makes electricity.

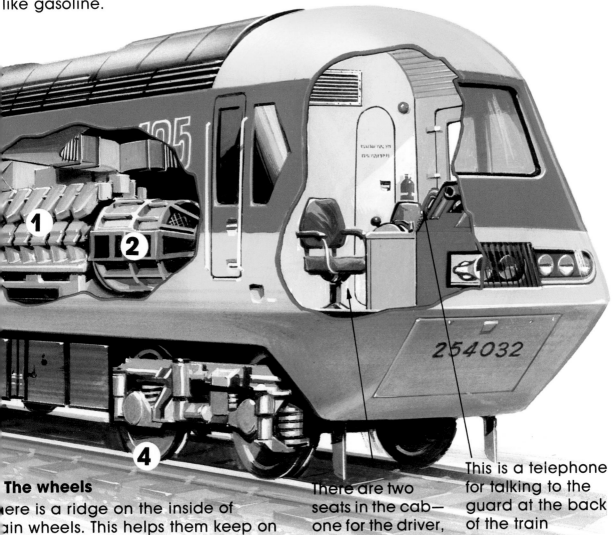

The wheels

ere is a ridge on the inside of
in wheels. This helps them keep on
e rails. The steel rails are fixed
sleepers made of wood or concrete.

There are two
seats in the cab—
one for the driver,
and one for the
co-driver.

This is a telephone
for talking to the
guard at the back
of the train

Bicycles

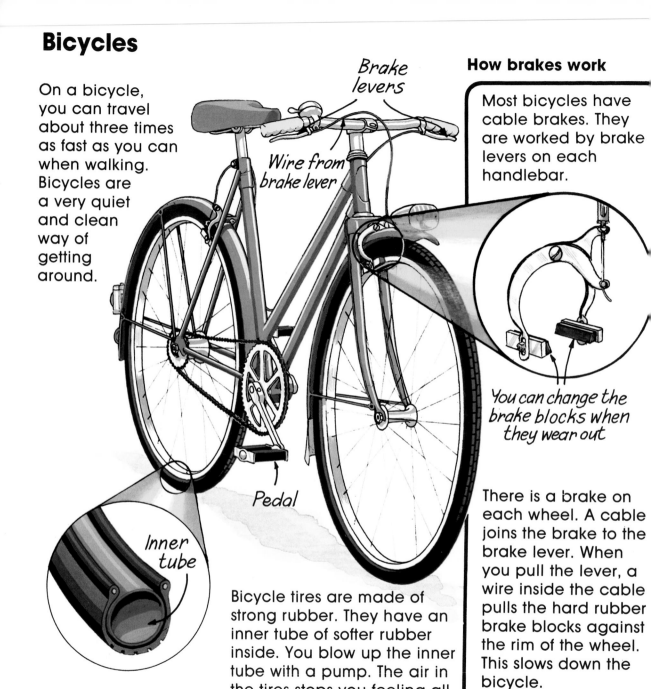

On a bicycle, you can travel about three times as fast as you can when walking. Bicycles are a very quiet and clean way of getting around.

Brake levers

Wire from brake lever

Pedal

Inner tube

Bicycle tires are made of strong rubber. They have an inner tube of softer rubber inside. You blow up the inner tube with a pump. The air in the tires stops you feeling all the bumps in the road.

How brakes work

Most bicycles have cable brakes. They are worked by brake levers on each handlebar.

You can change the brake blocks when they wear out

There is a brake on each wheel. A cable joins the brake to the brake lever. When you pull the lever, a wire inside the cable pulls the hard rubber brake blocks against the rim of the wheel. This slows down the bicycle.

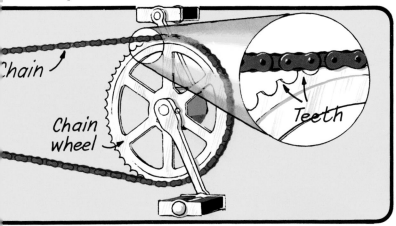

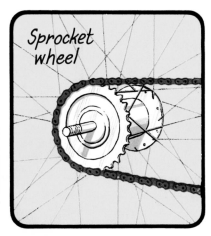

e pedals are fixed to a large chain wheel. When u push on the pedals the chain wheel goes round. e chain fits over the teeth of the chain wheel, so en the chain wheel is turned, the chain is pulled und.

At the back of the bicycle, the chain fits over a small sprocket wheel. This is joined to the back wheel.

e sprocket wheel goes round about three times ery time you pedal the chain wheel round once. is is because the chain wheel has about three nes as many teeth as the sprocket wheel.

The sprocket wheel turns the back wheel several turns for every one turn of the pedals.

Machines on a building site

There is a crane on the back of this truck. It can lift heavy things like iron girders and pipes.

At the end of th crane, which is fixed to the truc there is a moto This winds the steel cable and makes the hoo go up and dow

Bulldozers scrape the ground level and shovel up earth. A bulldozer needs tracks made of steel links to help it go along rough ground. These are turned by a powerful diesel engine.

Steel tracks

How a bulldozer turns

Bulldozer tracks cannot turn like the front wheels of a truck. If a bulldozer has to turn a corner, the driver makes the track on the outside of the curve go faster than the one on the inside. This pulls the bulldozer round.

This track goes fast

This track goes fast

These tracks go slower

This truck can mix concrete while it goes along the road. Cement, water and pebbles are put into the drum. The drum turns round and mixes them. When the truck arrives at a building site, the concrete is ready to use.

the past, big holes on ilding sites were dug lots of men using ovels. Now, a echanical digger can most of the work much icker. This digger has el legs which come wn at the front. These p the digger moving en it is digging.

Pistons

Steel legs

How a digger bucket works

To make the digger bucket move, thick oil is pumped along the digger arm into a cylinder. Inside the cylinder, the oil pushes a piston up and down. The piston is attached to a rod which pushes the bucket up and down.

Cylinder
Piston

Oil pushes piston along cylinder

Piston pushes bucket round

The parts of a car

This picture shows you the important parts of a car. We have taken away part of the car body, so you can see inside.

In most cars the engine is in the front and it makes the car go by turning the back wheels.

The gas tank

This is the tank which holds gas for the engine.

The springs

When you go over bumps in the road, the springs stop the passengers feeling the bumps.

The tires

Car tires are made of thick rubber. The tyres are filled with air. They have patterns, called treads, cut into them to help the car grip the road.

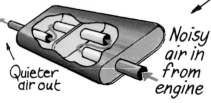

Quieter air out

Noisy air in from engine

The trunk

The trunk for carrying luggage is just above the gas tank.

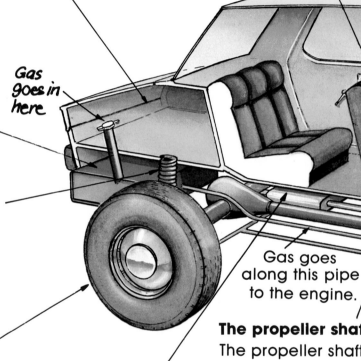

Gas goes in here

The muffler

The engine makes a lot of dirty smoke and noise. These go along the exhaust pipe and through the muffler. The muffler takes away much of the noise.

The hand brake

This is the handbrake. used when the car is parked. When the car moving, the driver uses the foot brake.

Gas goes along this pipe to the engine.

Br.
pi

The propeller shaft

The propeller shaft is a long rod. It joins the engine to the back wheels and makes ther go round.

Propeller shaft

Back axle

58

e windshield

e windshield is made
extra strong glass, so it
l not break easily.

The battery

The battery provides
electricity to help
start the engine and
work the lights.

The brakes

There is a brake on each
wheel. The outside of the
brake goes round with the
wheel. Inside the brake
there are two pads.

When you press on the
brake pedal, a liquid in the
brake pipes makes the
pads press against the part
of the brake that goes
round the wheel.

Brake pipe

These pads
press
outwards

This part
goes round
with the
wheel

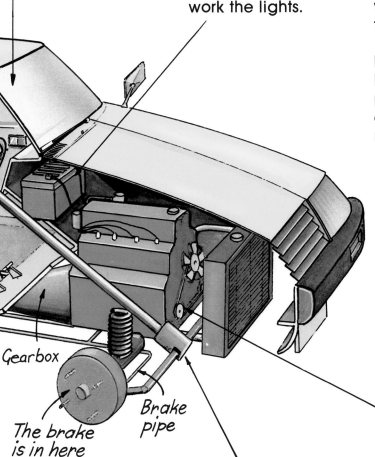

Gearbox

Brake
pipe

The brake
is in here

The engine

The engine makes the
wheels in the gearbox
turn round and these
make the propeller shaft
spin. This makes the back
axle spin and the back
wheels go round. You
can see how the engine
works on the next page.

e accelerator

hen you press down on
e accelerator pedal,
ore gas goes into the
gine and the car goes
ster.

The steering

To go round a corner,
you turn the steering
wheel to left or right. It is
linked to a rod which
turns the front wheels.

How a car engine works

Most cars have engines in the front, which make the back wheels go round.

Some cars have engines in the front, which make the front wheels go round.

Some cars have engine in the back, which mak the back wheels go round.

A car cylinder cut in half

Inside a car engine there are four or more metal tubes called cylinders. When the engine is working, a piece of metal called a piston goes up and down inside each cylinder. The picture below shows a cylinder cut in half.

Gas and air go in here

Spark plug

Exhaust gas comes out here

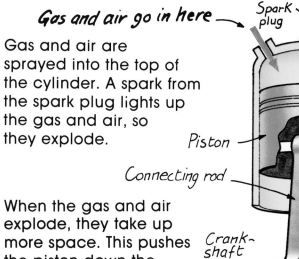

Piston

Connecting rod

Crank-shaft

Gas and air are sprayed into the top of the cylinder. A spark from the spark plug lights up the gas and air, so they explode.

When the gas and air explode, they take up more space. This pushes the piston down the cylinder.

The connecting rod connects the piston to the crankshaft. It swings from side to side in the bottom of the piston as the piston goes up and down.

The connecting rod make the crankshaft turn round.

The picture below shows a car engine with its side cut away so you can see how the pistons go up and down inside the cylinders. The pistons turn the crankshaft. The crankshaft turns the propeller shaft and this makes the back wheels go round.

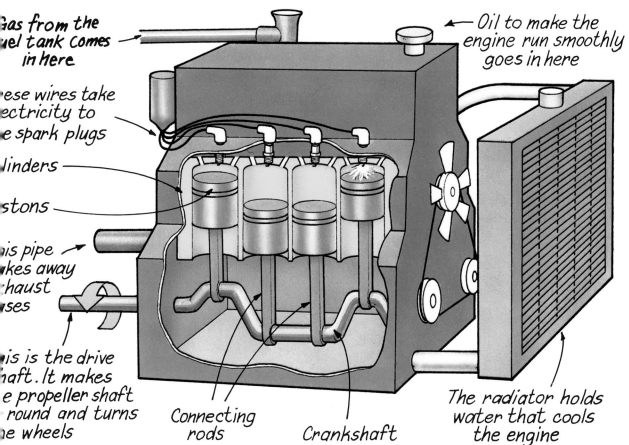

Gas from the fuel tank comes in here

These wires take electricity to the spark plugs

Cylinders

Pistons

This pipe takes away exhaust gases

This is the drive shaft. It makes the propeller shaft go round and turns the wheels

Connecting rods

Crankshaft

Oil to make the engine run smoothly goes in here

The radiator holds water that cools the engine

When gas and air explode in the top of the cylinders, they make the pistons go up and down. On the bottom of each piston is a connecting rod. This is joined to the crankshaft. When the pistons go up and down, they make the crankshaft turn the drive shaft round and round very fast.

The story of things that go

1

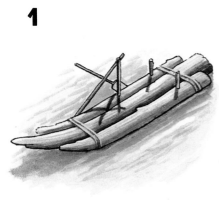

The earliest boat was made from a log. Later, several logs were tied together to make a raft.

2

5,000 years ago, the Egyptians made boats from reeds. These were used for carrying grain.

3

The wheel was invente over 4,000 years ago. I made it much easier t move heavy objects.

7

In 1820 the first bicycle was made from wood. It had no chain and was called a hobby horse.

8

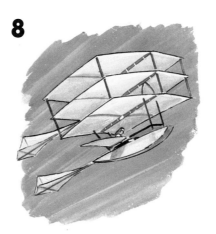

The first plane to fly was a glider built in 1852. The passenger was a ten year old English boy.

9

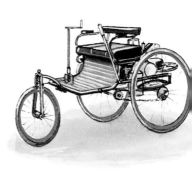

The first car driven by gas engine was made by Karl Benz in Germar in 1885.

5

6

e first submarine was ade of wood. It was built an American in 1775 d could only carry e man.

The first boat with an engine was made in France in 1783. Its steam engine worked two paddle wheels.

Early trains were steam trains. The first steam locomotive pulled a train in 1804.

11

12

1903 the first plane to y with an engine was uilt by the Wright rothers in the U.S.A.

The first jet plane to fly was the Heinkel He 178. It was made in Germany in 1939.

The first rocket to carry a person into space was the Russian Vostok. It was launched in 1961.

How fast do they go?

On this page you can compare the speeds of the different vehicles in this book.

The letters km/h used on this page are short for 'kilometers per hour'.

A kilometer is the distance you would walk if you walked at an ordinary speed for about 10 minutes.

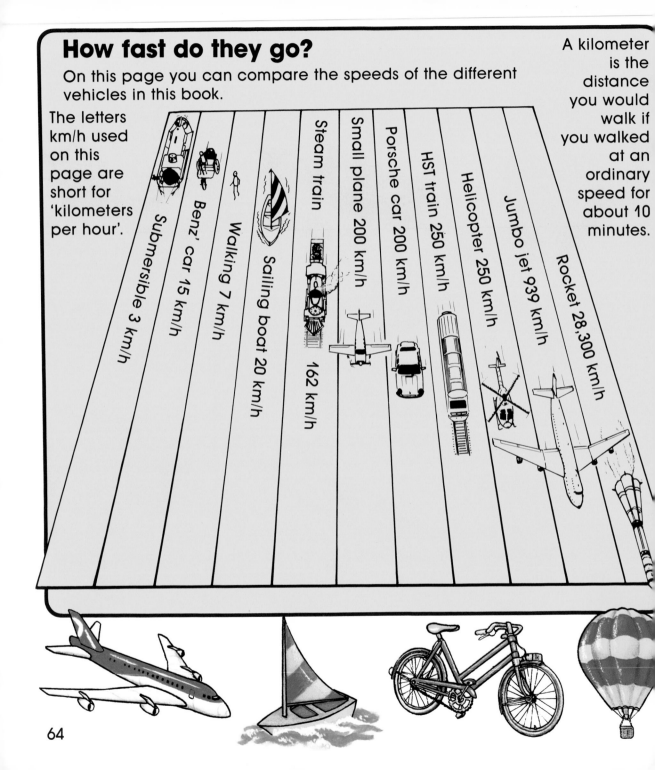

Submersible 3 km/h

Benz' car 15 km/h

Walking 7 km/h

Sailing boat 20 km/h

Steam train 162 km/h

Small plane 200 km/h

Porsche car 200 km/h

HST train 250 km/h

Helicopter 250 km/h

Jumbo jet 939 km/h

Rocket 28,300 km/h

Part 3

THINGS AT HOME

Written by: **Eliot Humberstone**
Designed by: **Iain Ashman and Sarah Simpson**

Consultant Editor **Betty Root**
Science Consultant: **Anthony Wilson**

Researcher: **Judy Allen**
Illustrated by:
Basil Arm
Louise Nevett
Sarah Simpson
Graham Smith
Guy Smith

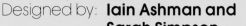

Contents

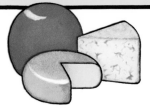

How a telephone works

1 Every telephone has its own number. When you dial a number, an electric message tells the telephone exchange which phone to ring.

Electric signals carry voices along this wire.

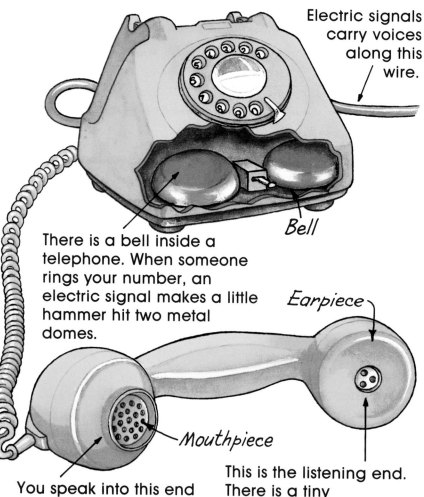

There is a bell inside a telephone. When someone rings your number, an electric signal makes a little hammer hit two metal domes.

Bell

Earpiece

Mouthpiece

You speak into this end and the microphone turns your voice into an electric signal.

This is the listening end. There is a tiny loudspeaker inside. It can turn electric signals back into sounds.

2

When you speak, the air from your mouth shakes the air around you. Each sound shakes the air in a different way.

5

At the telephone exchange, machines send the signals to the phone number you want.

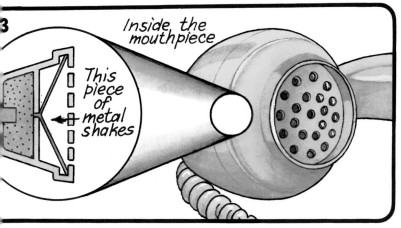
Inside the mouthpiece

This piece of metal shakes

ere is a thin piece of metal in a telephone
outhpiece. Each word you say shakes it in a
fferent way. It is this part of a microphone that
anges sounds into electrical signals.

Electric signals which
carry voices go along
wires to a telephone
exchange.

Underwater cable

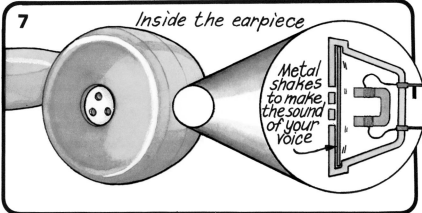
Inside the earpiece

Metal shakes to make the sound of your voice

ires at the bottom of the
a or satellites up in the
y carry telephone
gnals over long
stances.

In the earpiece of a telephone is a loudspeaker.
Electric signals make the magnet in a loudspeaker
pull and release a metal plate. The metal shaking
makes the sound of the other person's voice.

How a television works

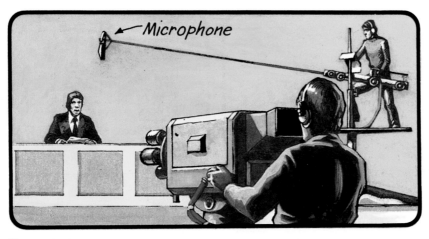

The picture you see on your TV is filmed by a special camera. This can be a long way away. The camera turns pictures into an electric signal. The microphone picks up sound which is turned into more electric signals.

The signals go along a cable to a TV transmitter. Pictures and words are sent out through the air like invisible messages.

A TV will not work well without an aerial. It can be fixed on to the roof of your house, or a small one can stand on the TV. The aerial picks up messages from the transmitter and sends them to the TV set.

When you switch on your set, it turns the signals in the wire back into sound and pictures.

Inside a television

The signal from the television transmitter is picked up by the aerial. It goes through a wire to the inside of the set.

The weak signal is made stronger in the amplifier.

The picture part of the signal goes into three electron guns. These point beams of electricity at the back of the screen.

Aerial

Electron guns

Phosphor patches

Loudspeaker

The sound part of the signal goes to the loudspeaker. It changes electricity back into sound.

The colors you see are made up of tiny patches of red, blue and green. They are so small that they merge together when you look at them.

The back of the screen is covered with thousands of tiny patches of a chemical called phosphor. When electricity hits this phosphor, the patches glow red, blue or green.

69

How bread is made

Bread is made from the seeds of the wheat plant. Wheat grows where there is plenty of sun and rain.

When the wheat is ripe, it is cut by a combine harvester. It is then sent to a flour mill.

At the mill, machines crush the wheat into a fine powder called flo[ur]

At the bakers

First the dough is mixed in a mixing machine.

This person is makin[g] the pieces of dough into loaves.

This woman is cutting dough into loaf-sized pieces.

make bread, you
ix fat, salt, water and
east with the flour. This
akes a dough.

The yeast makes the
dough rise. When it has
risen, it is put into a hot
oven to bake.

The dough turns into
bread after being baked
for about an hour. It is
taken out and left to cool.

The loaves are put on
trays and then they are
put in the oven to bake.

The fresh bread is ready
to be taken to the shop.

he loaves are left on
acks to rise. Bowls of
vater below help
eep the air damp.

Milk and cheese

1 Most milk comes from cows. Cows can only make milk if they eat enough fresh grass and drink enough water. Cows drink about 60 liters of water a day.

2 A cow makes milk to feed her calf. The calf sucks milk from a teat o the cow's udder.

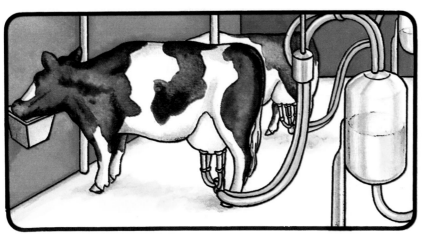

3 The milk we drink is taken from the cow by a machine. This sucks the milk out. The milk goes into a tank to be cooled. Often the cow eats food while she is being milked.

4 A tanker takes milk from the farm to the dairy. The tanker is insulated to keep the m cool.

When the tanker arrives at the dairy, the milk is unloaded. It is pumped out through a long hose.

6 Most milk is pasteurized. This means it is heated up and then cooled down quickly. This kills all the germs.

7 The pasteurized milk is put into bottles or cartons. Now it is ready for people to buy.

How cheese is made

Cheese is made from milk. It is mixed with rennet, a chemical from the lining of a cow's stomach.

The rennet makes the milk into a thick curd. Salt is added and the curd is packed into molds.

The curd is stored in a cool place. After about four months, it turns into cheese.

Cameras and films

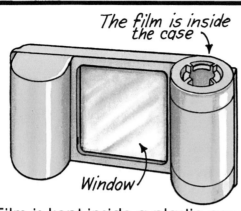

The film is inside the case

Window

Film is kept inside a plastic case. This kind of case has a square window in the middle. Light can only get to the part of the film which is in the window.

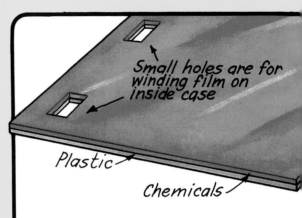

Small holes are for winding film on inside case

Plastic

Chemicals

The film is made of very thin plastic. It is covered on one side with chemicals. When light shines on the chemicals, it make an invisible picture on the film.

Negative picture on film

After you have finished taking your film, you send it to be developed. Developed film looks like this. The picture is called a negative because it is the opposite of the photograph you will get in the end.

You put the negatives in here

You put a negative film into an enlarger and shine light through it on to a piece of photographic paper. This makes the finished photograph.

Inside a camera

The picture below shows a simple camera. It is cut away so that you can see how it works.

You press this button to take a picture. It makes a shutter open and close. The shutter is a small metal plate behind the lens.

You wind on the film after you have taken a picture. A new piece of film is then in the window of the case.

3 The shutter opens for a moment and lets in light. Then it closes again. When the light shines in, it makes an invisible picture on the film.

4 This is the lens, it is a curved piece of glass. This makes light rays from in front of the camera make a clear picture on the film at the back of the camera.

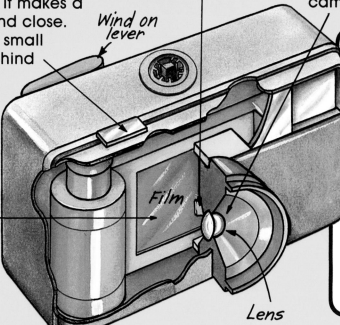

Wind on lever

Film

Lens

What the lens does to light

With a magnifying glass, you can use light from a window to make an upside-down picture like a camera lens does.

After taking the pictures

When you have used up all the film, you have to take it out of the camera. Some films take 12 and some take as many as 36 pictures.

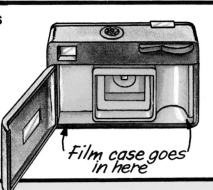

Film case goes in here

To take the film out, you open up the back of the camera. Then you send the film away to be developed and printed.

Light bulbs and flashlights

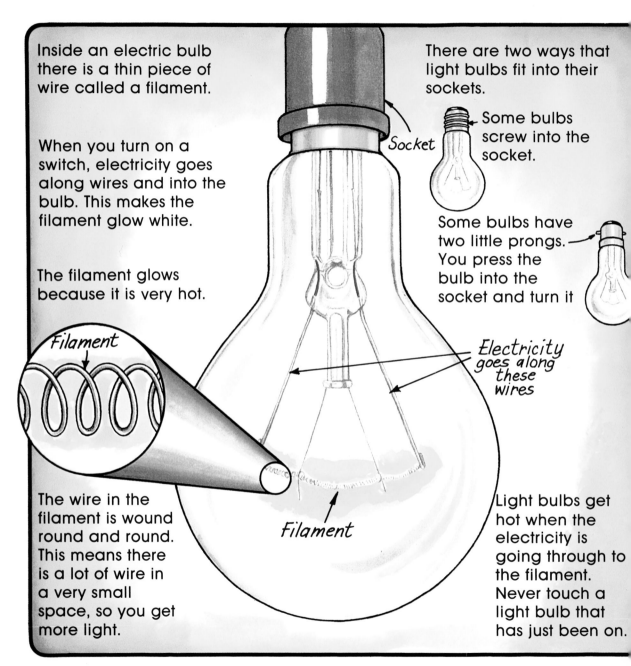

Inside an electric bulb there is a thin piece of wire called a filament.

When you turn on a switch, electricity goes along wires and into the bulb. This makes the filament glow white.

The filament glows because it is very hot.

Filament

The wire in the filament is wound round and round. This means there is a lot of wire in a very small space, so you get more light.

There are two ways that light bulbs fit into their sockets.

Socket

Some bulbs screw into the socket.

Some bulbs have two little prongs. You press the bulb into the socket and turn it

Electricity goes along these wires

Filament

Light bulbs get hot when the electricity is going through to the filament. Never touch a light bulb that has just been on.

Inside a flashlight

Flashlights work like ordinary lights in your home. They use electricity from the batteries inside.

Inside a battery there are chemicals that make electricity.

The flashlight only lights up if the electricity flows through both batteries. It goes to the bulb and back to the bottom of the batteries again. That is why there are strips of metal in the sides of the flashlight for the electricity to flow along.

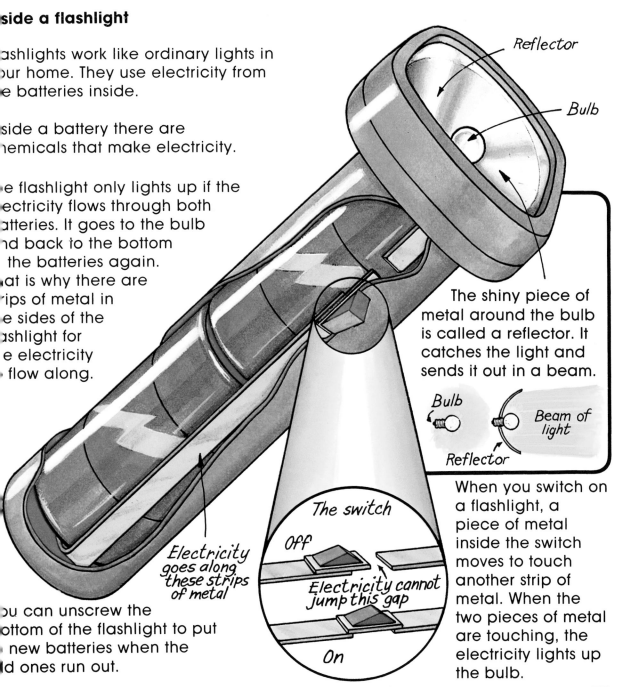

Reflector

Bulb

The shiny piece of metal around the bulb is called a reflector. It catches the light and sends it out in a beam.

Bulb

Beam of light

Reflector

Electricity goes along these strips of metal

The switch

Off

Electricity cannot jump this gap

On

You can unscrew the bottom of the flashlight to put in new batteries when the old ones run out.

When you switch on a flashlight, a piece of metal inside the switch moves to touch another strip of metal. When the two pieces of metal are touching, the electricity lights up the bulb.

How a stove works

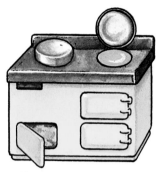

Not all stoves use electricity to make them hot. The one above uses coal. The one below uses gas.

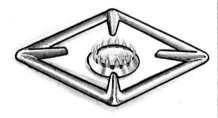

You can cook food out of doors on a barbecue grill. Barbecues burn charcoal which is made from partly burnt wood.

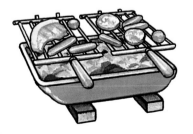

How an electric stove works

Inside the metal rings on top of an electric stove, there is a wire called an element. When you turn on the stove, electricity goes through the element. This makes the element very hot. There is a special powder around the element to stop the electricity getting to the metal ring.

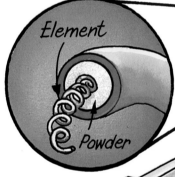

Element

Powder

Electric stoves have a thermostat connected to the oven switch. When the oven is hot enough, the thermostat turns off the electricity.

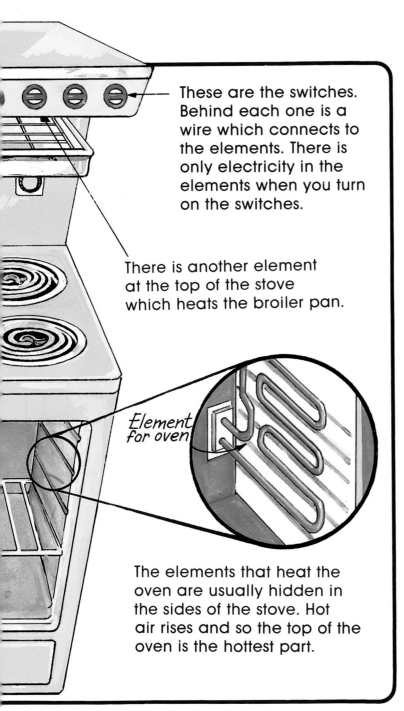

These are the switches. Behind each one is a wire which connects to the elements. There is only electricity in the elements when you turn on the switches.

There is another element at the top of the stove which heats the broiler pan.

Element for oven

The elements that heat the oven are usually hidden in the sides of the stove. Hot air rises and so the top of the oven is the hottest part.

The earliest way of cooking food was to put it on an open fire.

Before stoves were invented, people used to cook food in pots over fires.

The most modern electric stoves are called microwave stoves. They can bake a potato in about two minutes.

Keeping things cold

Everywhere around us there are thousands of tiny living things, too small for you to see. If you leave food out in the air they start to grow on it and you can see them as mold.

These tiny living things do not like the cold. We put food in the fridge to help stop it going bad.

In the past, ice was used to keep food cool. Farmers made ice by flooding their fields in winter. The fields froze and they collected the ice.

People used to keep food in larders. These were small rooms with cold stone floors. These helped keep the food cool so it stayed fresh longer.

;ide a refrigerator

Refrigerators keep
ngs cold because they
sh the warm air out at
e back.

At the back
ere are lots
pipes.

Inside the pipes
a liquid. The
uid turns to gas
it goes along
e pipes. When it
es this, it takes
vay the heat
m the food in
e fridge. This
akes the food
ooler.

The gas goes into
is compressor. It is
en turned into a
uid. Heat comes
ut when the gas
rns to liquid. You
n sometimes feel
e heat at the back
the fridge.

Warm air comes
out at the
back

2 Fridges are airtight to help keep
out warm air. A fridge door must
not be left open.

6 Now the liquid is ready
to go through the pipes
again and take away
more heat from the food.

7 When the food is cool
enough, a thermostat
switches the compressor off
until it is needed again.

81

Watches

Inside a watch there are lots of small wheels. After you wind up the watch, a spring unwinds and makes the wheels go round. The hour hand is attached to a wheel that goes round once an hour. The minute hand is joined to a faster wheel that goes round once a minute.

The numbers a
stuck on a piec
of tin. This go
between the whee
and the gla

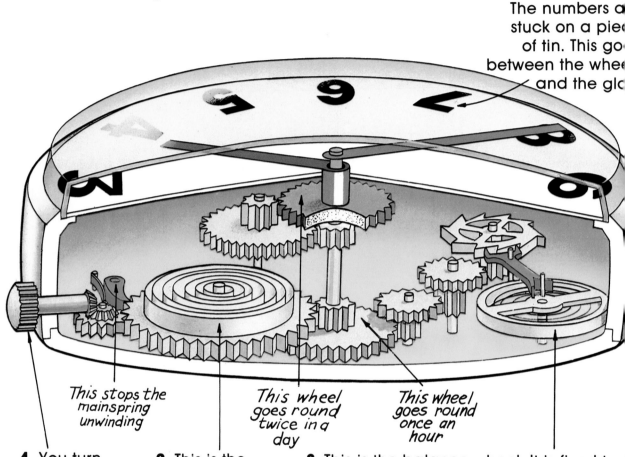

This stops the
mainspring
unwinding

This wheel
goes round
twice in a
day

This wheel
goes round
once an
hour

1 You turn this knob to wind up the mainspring.

2 This is the mainspring. As it unwinds, it turns round the wheel to which it is attached.

3 This is the balance wheel. It is fixed to spring that makes it go backwards and forwards. As the balance wheel turns, it makes the lever keep the escape wheel going round at a steady speed.

Inside a digital watch

Digital watches do not have moving hands. They show the time with changing numbers instead of springs and wheels, they work by using electricity from a tiny battery. This goes through a tiny quartz crystal and makes it shake over 30,000 times a second.

An electronic counter counts how many times the crystal shakes. Because the crystal shakes at a very even speed, the counter can work out how many seconds, minutes and hours are going by. It can then make the digits change so they show the right time.

This battery sends electricity to the tiny quartz crystal.

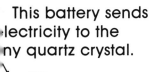

Electric messages go along these wires

Electricity makes the quartz crystal shake very fast.

3 Electronic counter counts how many times the crystal shakes and sends an electric message to the watch face.

How the numbers are made

On some digital watches you can see very faint figures of 8

The lines are made of a special material that goes dark when electricity comes to it. Each message from the electronic counter makes different lines go dark so you see different numbers every minute.

Try arranging seven matchsticks and you will see how you can make any number from 0 to 9.

83

Water, taps and toilets

Clean water
Comes in here

Dirty water
Comes out her

The water we use comes from rain. The rain soaks into the ground and runs into lakes and rivers.

Water is collected from rivers and stored in huge artificial lakes called reservoirs.

After it is cleaned, wate from the reservoir come through pipes under th ground into your home

How taps work

When the washer is up, water can flow out of the pipe. When you turn off the tap the washer goes down and stops water coming out of the pipe.

Taps are joined to metal pipes in the walls. Inside the tap there is a rubber washer. When you turn on the tap the washer comes up.

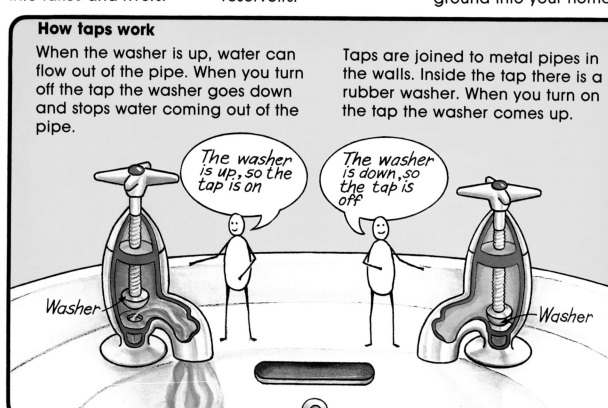

Water from drains goes to pipes underground. These pipes go to sewage works.

At the sewage works, water is cleaned with chemicals. It can now go back into the rivers.

After it has gone into the rivers, water can be collected in the reservoirs and used again.

What happens when you flush the toilet?

The tank above a toilet is called a cistern. It holds the water which is flushed into the bowl when you push the handle down. After it is flushed, the cistern fills with water again.

When you push the handle down, the plunger in the cistern forces water into the bowl below. The ballcock that floats on the water goes down. This makes more water go into the cistern.

Cistern

Ballcock

Water goes down this pipe

The plunger is worked by the handle

Bowl

Water comes in here

The handle is down, so the plunger pushes up. This lets the water flush into the bowl

Dust and vacuum cleaners

Almost everywhere you go, there is dust in the air. You can sometimes see the dust particles floating in a room when the sun shines through a window. Dust makes things dirty.

Dust test

Every Saturday for four weeks put a sheet of paper somewhere it will collect dust.

4 Weeks   2 Weeks
  3 Weeks   1 Week

At the end of the fourth week, see how much dust you have.

What is dust?

There are lots of different things in dust. You can see some of them in the circle.

These things can be tiny bits of wool and cotton, people's hair, little pieces of skin or the stuffing from chairs.

Sometimes dirt from outside can be found in dust inside.

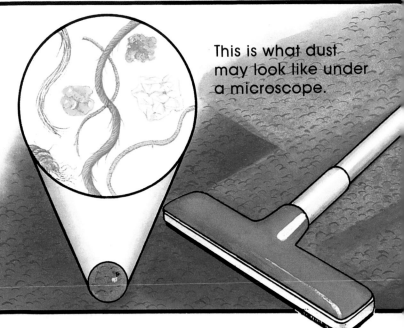

This is what dust may look like under a microscope.

low a vacuum cleaner works

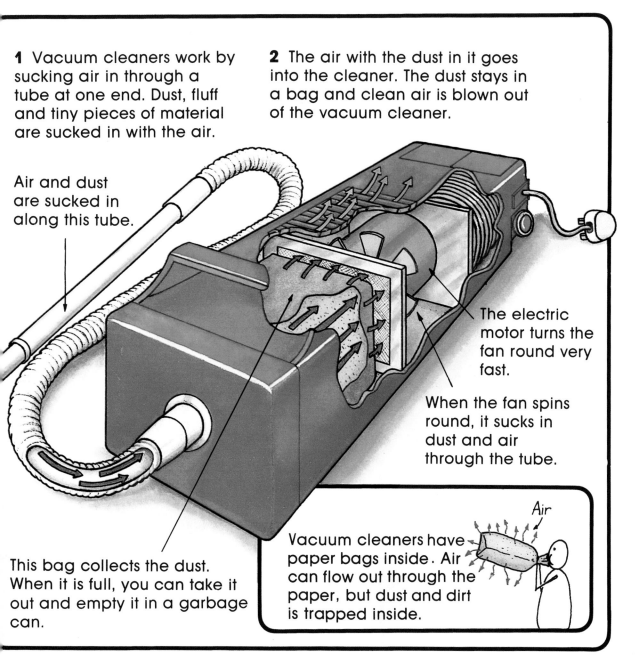

1 Vacuum cleaners work by sucking air in through a tube at one end. Dust, fluff and tiny pieces of material are sucked in with the air.

2 The air with the dust in it goes into the cleaner. The dust stays in a bag and clean air is blown out of the vacuum cleaner.

Air and dust are sucked in along this tube.

The electric motor turns the fan round very fast.

When the fan spins round, it sucks in dust and air through the tube.

This bag collects the dust. When it is full, you can take it out and empty it in a garbage can.

Vacuum cleaners have paper bags inside. Air can flow out through the paper, but dust and dirt is trapped inside.

Air

How glass is made

Glass is made from a special kind of sand called silica sand. It is often dug out of quarries.

The sand is mixed with other chemicals made from rocks. Then it is poured into a large furnace. The sand mixture is heated until it is so hot that it melts. It is called molten glass and is like soft toffee.

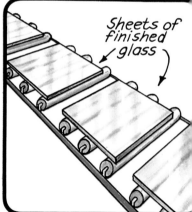

The molten glass is pulled out of the furnace. It is drawn through rollers to make it flat. It goes into another furnace and floats on hot liquid tin. As it moves across the tin, it cools and becomes harder.

After it has cooled down still more, the glass is hard and smooth and re to be cut to the right size

w bottles are made

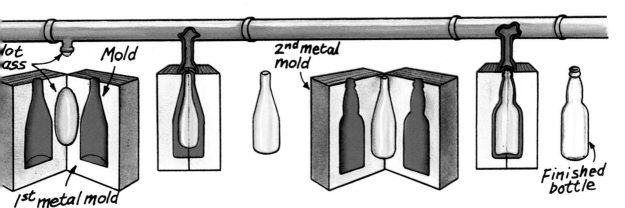

Hot glass

Mold

2nd metal mold

1st metal mold

Finished bottle

Molten glass from the furnace goes into a metal mold. The mold is shaped roughly like two halves of a bottle.

2 The mold closes and air is blown in. The air pushes the glass against the side of the mold. This makes it roughly bottle-shaped.

3 The glass goes into a second mold shaped like a finished bottle. The mold closes. Air is blown in and makes the bottle.

Glass blowing

Furnace

Some bottles and vases are still made by people and not by machines. They blow into a hot blob of molten glass. The glass can be turned on the end of a long pipe and blown into the right shapes.

How mirrors work

Protective paint

Glass   Metal

A mirror is a piece of glass that has been painted on one side with shiny metal. Underneath the silvery paint is a coat of protective paint.

Soap and washing machines

What soap does to water

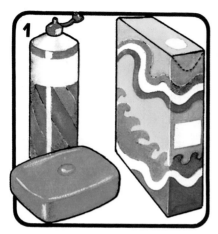

Soap is made up of millions of tiny parts called molecules. They are much too small to see.

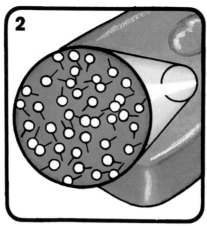

Each molecule has one part, the head, which loves water and another, the tail, which hates it.

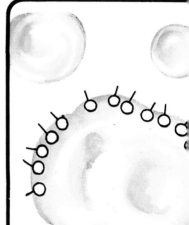

The tails of the soap molecules try to get out of the water. They break up the drops of water.

When you put dirty clothes into soapy water, the tails stick to the dirt to get away from the water.

The tails pull the dirt away from the cloth. This makes the cloth clean and the water dirty.

As the soapy water is broken up, it spreads out. Water without soap stays in drops.

How a washing machine works

this simple test to see
w soap changes
ater.

p a pencil in some
ean water. Shake the
ops onto a plate. Now
p the pencil in some
apy water and shake
e drops onto another
ate.

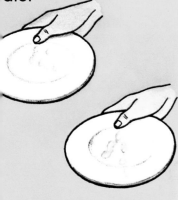

the plates a little and
u will see that the
ean water stays in
ops and the soapy
ater spreads out.

When you turn on a
washing machine, water
goes into the drum and
mixes with soap powder.
The clothes spin round in
the hot soapy water. This
takes out the dirt.

Hot and cold water goes
into the machine through
these pipes at the back.
The dirty water goes out
through the big grey
pipes at the bottom.

Soap powder
goes in here

Controls

Hot

Cold

Holes in the drum
let the water run
away so washing
can be rinsed

Electric
motor

There are heavy blocks of
concrete inside the
machine. These stop it
jumping about when the
drum spins round very
fast.

An electric motor drives a
belt that is attached to a
large wheel at the back
of the drum. This makes
the drum spin round.

How a cassette recorder works

The picture below shows a cassette tape recorder. Part of it has been cut away so you can see how it works.

This is the electric motor. It takes electricity from the batteries and makes the spindles go round so the tape goes past the tape head.

The batteries are kept in here. They store electricity that is needed for the motor, microphone and loudspeaker.

You do not need batteries if the recorder can be plugged into the electricity.

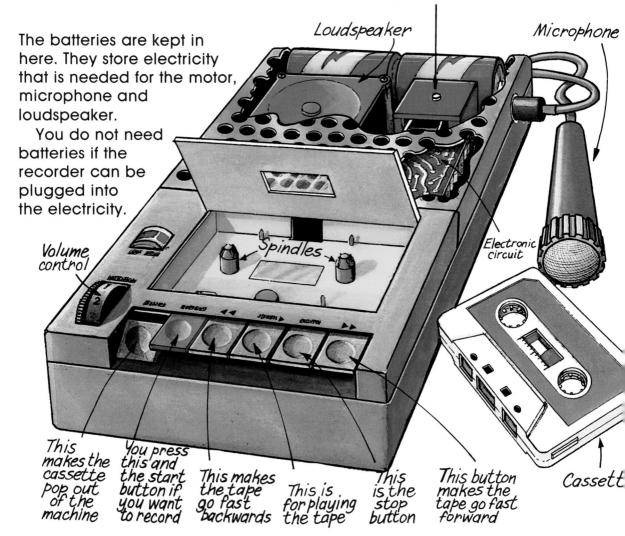

Loudspeaker

Microphone

Volume control

Spindles

Electronic circuit

Cassett

This makes the cassette pop out of the machine

You press this and the start button if you want to record

This makes the tape go fast backwards

This is for playing the tape

This is the stop button

This button makes the tape go fast forward

Two spools

Tape passes behind this window

here are two spools in a assette. When the corder is going, tape inds from one spool to e other.

Tiny magnets on the tape

The plastic tape is covered with thousands of tiny magnets that are too small to see.

Tape head pushes against the tape

When you play the tape, the magnets make electric signals in the tape head as they move past.

e electronic circuit ends electric signals to nd from the tape head.

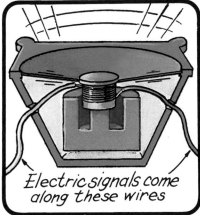

Electric signals come along these wires

The loudspeaker changes electric signals into the sounds of voices and music. This is what you hear.

Your voice makes part of the microphone shake

When you speak into the microphone, it turns your voice into an electric signal.

How this book was made

First we discussed what to write about. Then we researched and wrote about the different things.

Next we decided where the words and pictures should go. The designer drew rough plans for each page.

The drawings and the words were shown to children to make sure they could understand them.

Then the drawings were sent to an artist. She painted the pictures you can see in the book.

The words were sent to be typeset. This makes them easier to read than words from a typewriter.

The typeset words were stuck down around the pictures. The complete pages were then sent to the printers.

the printers

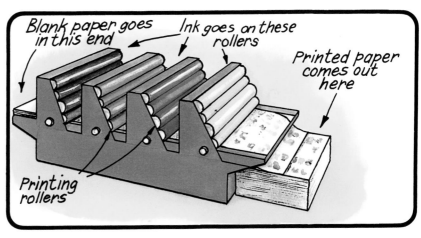

Blank paper goes in this end

Ink goes on these rollers

Printed paper comes out here

Finished printing plate

Printing rollers

s machine puts a picture the pages on to thin tal plates that are fixed to the printing machine.

Color books are actually printed with only four different colors—black, blue, red and yellow. Each sheet of paper is printed four times with a different printing plate for each color.

In the big circle you can see the tiny dots magnified

This machine staples the pages and the covers together

Finished books

k carefully at a color ture in a book. It is de up of lots of tiny s of ink.

The sheets of printed paper are folded so the pages are in the right order. They are cut to size and go on to a binding machine. This staples, sews or glues the pages together. Small books can have their covers stapled on. Some books have covers glued on.

Index

First published in 1981 by Usborne
Publishing Ltd, Usborne House,
83-85 Saffron Hill, London EC1N 8RT,
England. www.usborne.com

Copyright © 2007, 1987, 1981 Usborne
Publishing Ltd. Printed in Belgium. AE